COUNTRIES OF THE WORLD

Sweden

Gareth Stevens Publishing
A WORLD ALMANAC EDUCATION GROUP COMPANY

About the Author: Michele Wagner is a graduate of California State University, San Marcos. She works as a freelance writer and editor and enjoys reading, cooking, and traveling with her husband in her spare time.

PICTURE CREDITS

A.N.A. Press Agency: 71
Archive Photos: 58
Bes Stock: 18
T. Buckman: 79
Jan Butchofsky-Houser: 40
Camera Press: 3 (bottom), 9, 31, 36
    (bottom), 46, 47, 52, 53, 55, 56,
    66 (both), 80, 85
The Canadian Press Picture Archive: 75
    (Jockel Finck), 82 (Andrew Vaughan),
    83 (Chuck Stoody)
Embassy of Sweden: 14, 15 (top and
    center), 29 (both), 90 (both)
Focus Team – Italy: 7, 27
Peter Grant: 57
Blaine Harrington III: 22, 23, 25, 48,
    49 (bottom), 64, 65, 67, 91
Dave G. Houser: cover, 2, 4, 6, 19, 30, 32,
    33, 37, 42, 49 (top)
Hulton Getty/Archive Photos: 10, 11, 12,
    13, 15 (bottom), 50, 51, 54, 62, 76, 77,
    78, 84 (both)
The Hutchison Library: 21, 35
Imapress: 43
IMS Bildbyrå: 81
Tham Jan: 89
B. Klingwall: 20, 24, 45 (bottom)
Bosse Lind: 3 (center), 59
North Wind Picture Archives: 69
Hakan Pettersson: 16 (top)
Photobank: 1, 87
Roy Roberts: 17
Kay Shaw Photography: 74
Topham Picturepoint: 16 (bottom), 34, 36
    (top), 39, 44, 45 (top), 60, 61, 63, 68, 70
Trip Photographic Library: 3 (top), 5, 8, 26,
    28 (both), 38, 41
Vision Photo Agency: 72, 73

Digital Scanning by Superskill Graphics Pte Ltd

Written by
MICHELE WAGNER

Edited by
KATHARINE BROWN

Edited in the U.S. by
PATRICIA LANTIER
MONICA RAUSCH

Designed by
LOO CHUAN MING

Picture research by
SUSAN JANE MANUEL

First published in North America in 2001 by
Gareth Stevens Publishing
A World Almanac Education Group Company
330 West Olive Street, Suite 100
Milwaukee, Wisconsin 53212 USA

Please visit our web site at
www.garethstevens.com
For a free color catalog describing
Gareth Stevens' list of high-quality books
and multimedia programs, call
1-800-542-2595 (USA) or
1-800-461-9120 (CANADA).
Gareth Stevens Publishing's
Fax: (414) 332-3567.

© TIMES MEDIA PRIVATE LIMITED 2001
Originated and designed by
Times Editions
An imprint of Times Media Private Limited
A member of the Times Publishing Group
Times Centre, 1 New Industrial Road
Singapore 536196
http://www.timesone.com.sg/te

Library of Congress Cataloging-in-Publication Data
Wagner, Michele.
Sweden / Michele Wagner.
p. cm. — (Countries of the world)
Includes bibliographical references and index.
ISBN 0-8368-2340-0 (lib. bdg.)
1. Sweden—Juvenile literature. [1. Sweden.] I. Title.
II. Countries of the world (Milwaukee, Wis.)
DL619.5.W34   2001
948.5—dc21   2001020586

Printed in Malaysia

1 2 3 4 5 6 7 8 9 05 04 03 02 01

Contents

AN OVERVIEW OF SWEDEN

The Kingdom of Sweden is a country of contrasts and extremes. The country's varying landscapes include lowlands, highlands, rocky coasts, and sunny beaches. The long, freezing winters, when the days are as dark as the nights, are a stark contrast to the bright, glorious summers of the "land of the midnight sun."

A rich history filled with seafaring Vikings, strong kings, and a system of government studied the world over has helped shape modern Sweden. From Sweden's nearly two centuries of political neutrality to the excellence of its welfare system, the nation is unfamiliar with compromise. Today, Sweden has good trade and political relations with its neighbors and a position of prestige in the European Union (EU) and the United Nations (U.N.).

Opposite: **Stockholm's Gamla Stan, or Old Town, still retains the look and feel of the Middle Ages.**

Below: **These young Swedish folk dancers, dressed in traditional costume, wait their turn to perform in a competition held at Skansen, a historical, open-air museum in Stockholm.**

THE FLAG OF SWEDEN

The flag of Sweden is based on the Scandinavian Cross. The flag has a gold cross resting on a background of deep blue. The cross represents the country's Christian heritage, while the choice of blue and gold for the colors probably originated from the small Swedish coat of arms first used as a royal seal in 1364. Although officially adopted in 1906, the Swedish flag has a long history. Historians believe the flag was adopted in about 1520 as the standard under which the Swedish nationalists, headed by Gustav I Vasa, fought against King Christian II of Denmark.

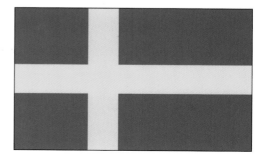

Geography

Sweden has an area of 173,686 square miles (449,964 square kilometers). It is the largest country in Scandinavia and the fourth largest in Europe. The Kjølen Mountains form a national border with Norway to the west and north. Finland lies to the northeast, and the long eastern coastline extends along the Gulf of Bothnia and the Baltic Sea. A narrow strait separates Sweden from Denmark in the far south.

Sweden has about 100,000 lakes and many rivers that make up nearly one-third of the country's area. More than half of Sweden's terrain is forested.

The land itself is generally divided into three major regions: Norrland, Svealand, and Götaland. Norrland, in the north, is the largest and least populated of the regions and makes up about three-fifths of the country. The area abounds in mountains, lakes, and river valleys. The far northern edge, beyond the Arctic Circle, overlaps the area of Lapland and is also home to Sweden's highest peaks, Mount Kebnekaise at 6,926 feet (2,111 meters)

ACID RAIN

One of Sweden's main environmental concerns is acid rain. Caused mainly by burning oil and coal, this type of pollution acidifies water sources and soils, endangers wildlife, and damages structures and monuments.
(A Closer Look, page 44)

Below: **Lapland is a northern region that covers parts of Norway, Sweden, Finland, and Russia. Forests of pine and spruce cover most of Swedish Lapland.**

Left: Stockholm, Sweden's capital city, is the country's most important center of commerce.

and Mount Sarektjåkkå at 6,854 feet (2,089 m). The country's chief rivers originate in the northern mountains and flow mainly southeast through the country, emptying into the Gulf of Bothnia or the Baltic Sea. These rivers include the Muonio River and the Torne River, both of which form a natural border with Finland.

Svealand runs through central Sweden and is a great expanse of lowland in the east and highland in the west. Stockholm, the country's capital, is located in the eastern part of this region. The eastern and western coastlines are rocky and flanked by hundreds of small islands. This region also contains Sweden's largest lakes, including Lake Vänern and Lake Vättern.

Götaland occupies the southern end of Sweden. This region contains the Småland Highlands and the fertile plains of Skåne County. Skåne is Sweden's oldest settled and most densely populated agricultural region, with over 70 percent of the land under cultivation. Göteborg, the country's principal seaport, is located in the western part of Götaland. The large, flat islands of Öland and Gotland are situated off the southeastern coast in the Baltic Sea.

THE PEARL OF THE BALTIC

Gotland is an island located in the Baltic Sea, about 56 miles (90 km) from the Swedish mainland. The island measures about 1,212 square miles (3,139 square km). Archaeological findings show that people have lived on the island for over 7,000 years. Today, about 60,000 people reside on Gotland, but that number rises to nearly one million in summer. Gotland is often called "the pearl of the Baltic" because of the island's gentle climate, natural beauty, and imposing monuments.

Climate

Sweden enjoys a pleasant climate, despite its northerly location. Low-pressure winds from the southwest blow in air warmed by the North Atlantic Current. These winds make the weather mild but changeable.

Above: In spring, wildflowers, such as these in a field in Uppsala, bloom throughout the country.

Summer temperatures average between 59° and 63° Fahrenheit (15° and 17° Celsius), and the days are usually clear and sunny. From May to July, the sun does not set completely for the 15 percent of the country that lies within the Arctic Circle. This area is known as the land of the midnight sun. The rainy season begins in late summer. The western slopes of southern Sweden receive more than 40 inches (102 centimeters) of rainfall a year, while the eastern coast has less than 28 inches (71 cm).

In winter, the temperatures are much lower in the north than in the south. The north receives heavy snowfall for nearly eight months of the year, and temperatures fall to as low as -40° F (-40° C). The south, however, has irregular snowfall, and temperatures average about 23° to 32° F (-5° to 0° C). In the northernmost part of the country, the land has nearly twenty hours of darkness a day.

Plants and Animals

Forests of pine, birch, and fir cover much of Sweden. Mixed forests are more common in the south, and deciduous trees, including beech, oak, ash, maple, and elm, are predominant in the far south. The forests abound with all types of mushrooms and berries, which anyone is entitled to pick and enjoy.

In the north, coniferous trees give way to mountain birches that extend to an elevation of 2,900 feet (884 m). The treeless mountains have marshes, heaths, and boulder fields that are home to alpine plant life, such as dwarf birch and willows.

Wolves used to be plentiful in Sweden but are now in danger of becoming extinct. Bears and lynx are common in the northern forests as are large herds of domesticated reindeer, herded by the Sami. Wolverines live in the mountains, while moose, roe deer, foxes, and hares thrive in most areas.

Birds are scarce in winter, but during summer, Sweden's many bodies of water attract great numbers of migratory birds, such as cranes and wild geese, from southern Europe and Africa. Fish species range from perch and carp to salmon, herring, and pike. These types of fish are found in the Baltic Sea, as well as in Sweden's many lakes and rivers.

THE WOLVERINE

The wolverine, a member of the weasel family, has long fascinated hunters, trappers, and animal lovers. Although a protected species in Sweden's cold, northwest region since 1969, this cunning and ferocious animal is in danger of extinction.
(A Closer Look, page 72)

Below: **Herds of domesticated reindeer thrive in the forests of Swedish Lapland.**

History

The first evidence of human life in Sweden dates back to about 9,000 B.C. By 6,500 B.C., a nomadic, food-gathering culture had developed. More tribes settled in the area around 2,500 B.C. These tribes relied on agriculture and also raised cattle. From A.D. 1, Sweden was inhabited by the Svear, or Suiones (Swedes), and the Gotär. Historians believe the Swedes were the dominant peoples by the ninth century.

By the end of the eleventh century, Christianity was the main religion, and Sweden began to unify as a nation ruled by a king. For two hundred years, civil wars and feuds raged as various claimants fought for the throne. Stability was eventually achieved in the mid-thirteenth century, with the emergence of the Folkung dynasty.

The Folkung Dynasty

Beginning with the rule of Birger Jarl in 1248, Sweden's economy flourished under the Folkung dynasty. Trade blossomed between Sweden and other parts of Europe, especially with the Hanseatic, or German, cities. Sweden's territorial boundaries were also expanded, and, by 1335, Magnus II, the last Folkung king, ruled Sweden, Finland, Norway, and Halland (now a Swedish county).

THE VIKINGS

From the ninth to the eleventh centuries, Vikings set sail from their homes in Sweden and raided countries throughout Europe in search of land, slaves, gold, and silver. The speed and daring of their attacks became legendary, and they were feared by peoples from all nations.
(*A Closer Look, page 68*)

THE END OF THE FOLKUNG DYNASTY

When Magnus II attempted to limit the economic and political power of the leading Swedish nobles, the Swedish nobility revolted and forced Magnus to give up his throne in 1363. However, his son, Haakon, married Margaret, the daughter of the Danish king, in the same year, paving the way for the Kalmar Union in 1397.

Left: This petroglyph, or cave painting, shows three figures holding axes. It was painted by a prehistoric tribe that inhabited Sweden during the Bronze Age. The painting is one of many that can be found at the Tanum Museum of Rock Carvings.

Left: Margaret I (1353–1412) became the undisputed ruler of Denmark, Norway, and Sweden in 1397, with the establishment of the Kalmar Union. She ruled the union until her death in 1412. Although each of the three countries in the union had its own laws and administration, Margaret skillfully centralized power.

The Kalmar Union

The Swedish nobility, unhappy with Magnus II, gave the throne to Albert of Mecklenburg in 1363. The nobility, however, disliked Albert's favorable policies toward Germany. They turned to Margaret I, regent of Norway and Denmark, for help. Her troops defeated Albert in 1389, and, in 1397, her great-nephew Erik of Pomerania was crowned king of Sweden, Denmark, and Norway, marking the beginning of the Kalmar Union. Margaret continued to rule as regent until her death. Erik officially succeeded her as monarch in 1412, but he lacked her diplomacy. His foreign policy led to the end of Sweden's overseas trade with the German cities, which, in turn, sparked an uprising in the Bergslagen district of Sweden. The mayhem that followed ended when the Danish and Swedish councils deposed Erik in 1438 and 1439, respectively. From then on, quarrels within each country and wars between Denmark and Sweden troubled the union until its dissolution in 1523.

THE RISE AND FALL OF SWEDEN'S INDUSTRIES

From A.D. 800 to the thirteenth century, the cultivation of Swedish land was continual, with over 90 percent of the population working in the agricultural sector. The mining industry was also very successful by the 1400s, and copper and iron were the most important exports from Sweden. In the first half of the fourteenth century, however, a plague called the Black Death swept the land, killing thousands of people. The country declined economically as well, and expansion ceased.

Left: During his reign, King Gustav I Vasa made the Catholic Church a national institution and seized much of its property.

GUSTAV I VASA

Considered by many Swedes as the founder of their nation, King Gustav I Vasa is credited with laying the foundations for Sweden's independence from the Kalmar Union.
(A Closer Look, page 50)

THE WARSHIP *VASA*

In 1628, the *Vasa* was considered a terrifying and ultra-modern war machine. The warship, however, sunk on her maiden voyage and lay undisturbed in a watery grave until 1961.
(A Closer Look, page 70)

THE THIRTY YEARS' WAR

Not only did Vasa kings fight wars over territorial boundaries, trade, and dynastic claims, they also drew Sweden into religious wars, such as the Thirty Years' War in Germany (1618–1648). The war was between the Holy Roman Empire and Protestant groups. With the signing of a peace treaty in the German province of Westphalia in 1648, Sweden gained control of the Baltic Sea.

The Vasa Dynasty

When Gustav I Vasa came to the Swedish throne in 1523, he defeated Denmark and broke away from the three-nation alliance. He began rebuilding the country by organizing a centralized administration, building up the army, and encouraging trade and industry. He also encouraged the spread of the Lutheran faith, which became the state religion in 1544.

His successors faced continuous struggles with the nobility, who wanted a constitutional government and more power. Furthermore, constant vying for power and dominance over trade routes resulted in nearly three hundred years of warfare with Denmark, Poland, Russia, and Germany.

The Napoleonic Wars

By the early nineteenth century, Sweden was embroiled in the Napoleonic wars. Sweden sided with Britain, Russia, and Austria in 1805. In 1807, however, Russia signed a peace agreement with France and, in 1808, supported the Danish invasion of Finland, which was under Swedish rule. Sweden suffered a humiliating defeat in 1809 and was forced to surrender Finland and the Åland Islands to Russia. In 1814, however, Sweden expanded its territory, when it defeated Danish troops and formed a union with Norway that lasted until 1905.

Sweden as a Neutral Power

Until the end of the nineteenth century, Sweden was mainly an agricultural country. By the end of the century, however, the nation had witnessed a rise in population and the beginning of industrialization and urbanization. Progress was also made in social legislation, including accident insurance for workers and the introduction of compulsory education.

As Sweden moved into the twentieth century, economic changes prompted political reform, including universal suffrage for men in 1907. Further social advancements were put on hold, however, following the outbreak of World War I in 1914. Throughout the war, Sweden remained neutral and sought to protect its economic interests.

After the war, the demand for Swedish products rose dramatically, and the nation enjoyed a period of economic prosperity until the Great Depression of 1929. In 1920, Sweden had furthered its non-aggressive policy by joining the League of Nations, an international organization established to peacefully settle disputes between nations. The following year marked a breakthrough in Swedish democracy, when all Swedes gained the right to vote.

THE BREAKUP OF THE UNION

The Swedish-Norwegian union was not a successful alliance. The only common ground between them was the joint monarchy and foreign policy. By the late nineteenth century, the union began to show serious signs of strain, as Norway resented its inferior status in the union. Gradually loosening its ties, Norway dissolved the union to become an independent nation in 1905.

Below: King Oscar II opened the Swedish parliament in June 1905 amid speculation that Norway was preparing to declare its independence.

Political Changes

During World War II, Sweden once again remained neutral, despite frequent border incidents and German attacks on Swedish shipping. After the war, Sweden gained membership to the U.N., without relinquishing its neutral foreign policy.

Until the mid-1970s, Sweden enjoyed strong economic growth and the emergence of an impressive welfare state program. In 1975, however, the country faced inflation and a large budget deficit, following the 1974–1975 world economic slump. Since then, successive governments have focused their attention on economic problems, such as unemployment and inflation.

In 1961, Sweden joined the European Free Trade Association (EFTA) and remained a member until 1994. Under the leadership of Ingvar Carlsson from the Social Democratic Party (SDP), however, the Swedish population voted to leave EFTA and become a member of the EU, a larger economic organization of European countries, on January 1, 1995.

SWEDEN AS A PROMOTER OF PEACE

Through two world wars and the international conflicts of the twentieth century, Sweden has continued to follow a policy of neutrality. To date, the country has refused to join the North Atlantic Treaty Organization (NATO), an organization that deals with the collective defense of Western powers. Swedish troops, however, play a leading role in U.N. peacekeeping operations. Sweden is also a member of the Nordic Council, which allows the free movement of people and trade among Scandinavian countries.

Left: The current king of Sweden is Carl XVI Gustaf. The king came to the throne in 1973 and acts as the official representative of the country. His consort is Queen Silvia.

Queen Kristina (1626–1689)

Kristina became queen-elect of Sweden before the age of six and was crowned queen in 1644, at age eighteen. Her mediating skills led to the Peace of Westphalia, which ended the Thirty Years' War. She also kept the heated class rivalries, which erupted in Sweden after the war, from lapsing into civil war. Called "Minerva of the North" for her wit and wisdom, Kristina was a keen patron of the arts. During her reign, science and literature flourished. Kristina also encouraged trade and the development of mining. In 1654, she abdicated and left for Rome to pursue the Roman Catholic faith, to which she had secretly converted.

Queen Kristina

Fredrika Bremer (1801–1865)

Credited with introducing the domestic novel into Swedish literature, Fredrika Bremer was born in Swedish Finland and moved to Sweden in 1804. Bremer was a reformer and champion of women's rights. Her first novel, *Familjen H.* (1831), brought her instant fame and popularity throughout Scandinavia. She traveled extensively, particularly to the United States, where she was welcomed because of her antislavery position. Upon her return to Sweden, she wrote *Hertha* (1856), in which she argued that women should work toward improving society. The book paved the way for major political and economic reforms that helped Swedish women.

Fredrika Bremer

Raoul Wallenberg (1912–1947?)

Born into a wealthy Swedish family, Raoul Wallenberg worked for a central European trading company. When Germany sent Nazi troops into Hungary to round up Jews and other "undesirables" in 1944, Wallenberg traveled to Budapest, Hungary, to save as many Hungarian Jews as possible from the Nazi concentration camps. It is estimated that he rescued between 4,000 and 35,000 Jews. At the end of the war, Wallenberg was taken prisoner by Russian troops. He allegedly died in a Russian prison cell in 1947. In 1981, the United States granted honorary citizenship to the missing Wallenberg.

Raoul Wallenberg

Government and the Economy

Sweden is a constitutional monarchy. The current constitution, adopted in 1809 and revised in 1975, is based on popular sovereignty, representative democracy, and parliamentary law.

Sweden's government consists of legislative, executive, and judicial branches. The *Riksdag* (RICKS-dahg), or legislative body, is a unicameral parliament made up of 349 members. Swedish voters elect 310 members of the Riksdag to four-year terms by voting for political parties in their local constituency. The remaining thirty-nine seats are distributed among the parties according to each party's proportion of the nationwide vote.

The speaker of the Riksdag nominates the prime minister after consulting party leaders. The nominee is then approved through a vote of parliament. The prime minister appoints the members of the cabinet. The cabinet is responsible for all government decisions. The current prime minister is Göran Persson. King Carl XVI Gustaf is the chief of state, but his duties are primarily ceremonial.

Above: **Reelected as prime minister in 1998, Göran Persson is a member of the SDP, Sweden's largest political party.**

Left: **The Riksdag building in Stockholm is the center of political life in Sweden.**

Sweden has three levels of courts: *tingsrätter* (TINGS-reh-ter), or district courts; *hovrätter* (HOVE-reh-ter), or intermediate courts of appeal; and *högsta domstolen* (hohg-stah DOOM-stoo-len), or Sweden's Supreme Court. District courts handle most cases and contain a panel of *nämndemän* (NEM-deh-men), or appointed assistants, who take part in hearings.

Local Government

Sweden is divided into 284 *kommuner* (koh-MOON-er), or municipalities. Each municipality has an elected assembly, with elections coinciding with parliamentary elections. The assemblies' primary responsibilities include water supply, public assistance, child welfare, housing, and care for the elderly. The country also is divided into 21 *län* (lehn), or counties. The national government appoints county governors and county administrative boards.

OMBUDSMEN

Originating in Sweden, the office of ombudsman has existed since 1809. Appointed by the Riksdag for a four-year term, the ombudsmen, or public officials, are responsible for ensuring that the courts, as well as central and local government authorities, correctly apply the rules to which they are subject. These public officials also investigate complaints made by citizens against government agencies or officials.

Left: **This car factory is located in Linköping. Almost half the cars made in Sweden are exported to the United States. Leading Swedish carmakers include Volvo and SAAB.**

The Economy

Sweden is a highly developed country with a steady, reliable economy. The country's gross national product (GNP) is one of the highest in the world, with taxes to match. Ninety percent of Swedish industry is privately owned, while government ownership is limited to mines, public transportation, and energy.

During the second half of the twentieth century, employment in forestry, agriculture, and fishing decreased. The services and administration sector has become the main area of growth, and the number of women in this part of the workforce is higher than in most countries. Service industries include education, health care, and trade.

Sweden's industries range from metals and engineering to electronics and communications. The construction and food-processing industries continue to be important, and pharmaceutical and biotechnology industries have expanded rapidly in recent years.

Most farmable land is found in southern Sweden, and wheat, barley, sugar beets, oilseeds, and potatoes are the main crops. Although hay and potatoes are grown in the northern part of the country, raising livestock, such as cows, pigs, and poultry, is more important. Swedish farms boast some of the highest yields in the world.

EMPLOYEE BENEFITS

Sweden is highly unionized and is noted for its liberal employee benefits plans. The minimum amount of annual paid vacation is five weeks and two days, and the actual working hours in Swedish industry are among the lowest in Europe.

Sweden is rich in mineral resources and has vast forests. A wide range of metals, such as gold, copper, lead, zinc, and iron, are mined. The country, however, lacks fossil fuels, such as petroleum, and relies heavily on imports to meet its needs.

The value of Sweden's exports amounts to 30 percent of its gross domestic product (GDP). Major exports include machinery, motor vehicles, paper products, pulp and wood, iron and steel products, and chemicals. Nearly half of Sweden's imports are engineering products. The other half is made up of petroleum and petroleum products, iron and steel, chemicals, and foodstuffs. The country's main export and import trading partners are Europe, the United States, and Norway.

Transportation

Sweden has an expansive system of land and air transportation routes. Nearly twenty ports handle foreign trade, with Stockholm

being one of the most important. Ferry traffic between Sweden and its neighbors is becoming more and more common.

Cars are the main form of land transportation, and Sweden's well-built and maintained roads make travel easy. Most households have at least one car. The local public bus systems are also well developed, but only Stockholm has a subway system.

Air services are dominated by Scandinavian Airlines (SAS), which is jointly owned by Sweden, Denmark, and Norway. Sweden's major airports are in Stockholm, Göteborg, and Malmö.

Above: The beautiful and vibrant city of Stockholm is best seen from the water.

People and Lifestyle

The Swedish population is unusually homogeneous in language, religion, and ethnic heritage because the majority of Swedes are of Germanic descent. The standard of living is high, and no official distinction is made between town and countryside, since they are joined administratively by the municipalities.

Most of the population lives in the southern half of Sweden, especially in the central lowlands, the plains of Skåne, and the coastal lowlands. The majority of Swedes live in cities but have homes in the countryside that they visit during vacations. The Swedish are a vibrant, colorful people who enjoy life, and they are known for their strength of character.

Throughout the centuries, many different groups have influenced Swedish culture, but no particular group stands above the others. Sweden has also had its share of immigration, with groups of people from countries such as the former Yugoslavia, Greece, Norway, Denmark, Turkey, and Chile settling in various parts of the country. Many of these people come as guest workers because of Sweden's good economy.

Below: **Although foreign-born people living and working in Sweden have added some diversity to the population, most Swedes have blond hair and blue eyes. These young people live in the city of Eskiltuna.**

Sweden has two minority groups of indigenous inhabitants — the Finnish-speaking peoples of the northeast along the Finnish border and the Sami.

Although Finns have migrated to Sweden since the sixteenth century, the bulk of the Finnish-speaking peoples arrived after World War II (1939–1945) and, in particular, in the late 1960s. Today, Finns in Sweden number 500,000. They work mainly in the industrial parts of the country, including the cities of Stockholm and Eskiltuna. The Finnish-speaking peoples of Sweden have managed to maintain their own identity. In fact, the Swedish government recently acknowledged that the Finns form a permanent minority group.

The Sami, sometimes referred to as Lapps, number around twenty thousand in Sweden, although they also live in the other Scandinavian countries. They were once a hunting and fishing people, but now they are mainly reindeer herders, miners, or forestry workers.

Above: **Many Swedes buy fresh produce from marketplaces set up around Stockholm and other Swedish towns and villages.**

THE SAMI

The Sami have an active organizational structure that preserves their culture and protects their rights. They are eager to make themselves heard in all arenas, especially in politics.
(A Closer Look, page 56)

21

Family Life

Sweden is a family-oriented country, and families play an important role in Swedish society. Family members gather to celebrate holidays and special occasions. Today, large families are rare since families tend to live in urban areas, where housing is in short supply. Consequently, Sweden has one of the lowest birth rates in the world.

The Swedish government places great emphasis on the value of family, and parents receive a monetary stipend from the government for every child. The workplace is also family-friendly. Quality day-care centers are provided for the children of working mothers, and, by law, parents can take time off work to care for their children.

Since the mid-twentieth century, Sweden has come to realize the importance of the family unit. Unmarried mothers, therefore, are more fortunate in Sweden than in many other industrialized countries. The government provides approximately the same benefits to an unmarried mother that a married woman receives from her husband. For example, the absentee father of a child, by law, has to pay a monthly amount toward the mother's and child's expenses. If he cannot be located, Sweden's child welfare board supplies the funds.

Above: Swedish parents can obtain low-cost loans from the government to provide a home for their children. The government also provides a tax-free allowance for all children under the age of sixteen.

THE SWEDISH WELFARE STATE

The introduction of the Swedish welfare state has been a main factor in allowing the Swedes to enjoy one of the highest standards of living in the world.
(*A Closer Look, page 64*)

Swedish families also take great care of their elderly relatives. Although most elderly people live alone or with their spouse, their children and extended family play a large role in their lives. The government reinforces this attitude by providing its elderly citizens with a comprehensive public health care system, as well as substantial housing subsidies.

Despite the country's respect for family unity, however, Sweden has one of the highest divorce rates in Europe. The reasons for this high rate may include the declining influence of the Church of Sweden, the easy accessibility of obtaining a divorce, and the growing emancipation of women.

Women

Since the end of World War II and the establishment of inexpensive, state-funded day-care centers, an increasing number of women have joined the workforce. Today, most Swedish women work outside the home.

Left: Younger family members often spend a great deal of time with their elderly relatives.

SWEDISH WOMEN

Swedish women have worked hard to establish their rights in the country's political, social, and economic arenas. Today, women in Sweden work in all sectors except the armed forces.
(*A Closer Look, page 66*)

Education

Sweden's educational system is organized, effective, and of a high caliber. Education is public and free to all. Elementary and high schools are run by the municipalities. Universities and colleges are administered by the state but have a great deal of freedom in exercising their resources. Today, at 99 percent, Sweden has one of the highest literacy rates in the world.

The majority of Swedish children attend preschools when they reach six years of age. Students normally begin *grundskola* (GRUND-school-ah), or elementary school, at the age of seven, but some children start at the age of six. Elementary school is compulsory for nine years.

Sami-speaking children can attend Sami schools that offer an ethnically adapted education program that corresponds to the first six years of compulsory school. Special schools also exist for children with mental and physical disabilities.

Sweden also has privately owned, independent schools that are open to all and approved by the National Agency for Education. About 2 percent of the country's elementary school students attend independent schools.

ENGLISH AS A SECOND LANGUAGE

In Sweden, every elementary school student between the ages of nine and thirteen is required to learn English as a second language. About ninety percent of students continue studying English after this compulsory period.

Left: These two students attend elementary school in Eskiltuna.

Above: **Today, some Swedish high school students still maintain the Scandinavian tradition of wearing ceremonial white hats at graduation.**

Grundskola is divided into three-year stages: lower, middle, and upper. All students follow the same curriculum for the first six years. English is introduced in the third year, and other languages can be studied in the following years. Beginning in the seventh year, students can choose their own subjects. A new national curriculum was introduced in 1994 and offers a wide variety of subjects, including geography, history, religious education, sciences, art education, and music.

High school, or *gymnasieskola* (jim-NAH-zee-eh-school-ah), is voluntary and free, and students begin it at age sixteen. Nearly 90 percent of students attend high school. The curriculum is divided between university-oriented and job-oriented programs. Sixteen programs are available, and all last for three years. All programs include English, art, mathematics, natural science, civics, Swedish, and religious education.

Sweden has thirteen universities, the oldest of which is the University of Uppsala, founded in 1477. Higher education is free, but only about 30 percent of students go on to pursue further studies.

Left: **Many simple but beautifully designed churches can be found in Gamla Stan, or Stockholm's Old Town.**

Religion

Sweden's national religion is Lutheranism, which was adopted around the mid-sixteenth century. Today, about 90 percent of the population belongs to the Evangelical Lutheran Church of Sweden. Of this figure, only 10 percent attends church services regularly.

Most Swedes go to church only on Christmas, Easter, and Advent Sunday and for major events, such as christenings, baptisms, and weddings. The majority of the population has a relaxed attitude toward religion but still recognizes the church as an important preserver of tradition.

For many years, the Lutheran Church was a state church, which meant that every Swede automatically became a member at birth if one of his or her parents was a member. The church was also a central part of state administration. Gradually, however, the church began to separate from the state and, in 1996, gained full independence. Today, children must be baptized to become members of the church.

THE SWEDISH REFORMATION

Until the sixteenth century, Sweden was Roman Catholic, with the church controlling the government and most of the land. When Gustav I Vasa came to power in 1523, he loosened the church's stranglehold and reclaimed most of its land. His actions caused unrest and eventually led to Gustav's rejection of Roman Catholicism and adoption of the Lutheran faith by 1544.

Apart from the Lutheran Church, several other faiths and sects exist in Sweden; however, most of them are small. Other religions include Roman Catholicism, Islam, Buddhism, Judaism, and Hinduism. In addition, religious communities of Mormons, Pentecostals, and Jehovah's Witnesses are located throughout the country.

Folk Beliefs

Sweden is rich in folk beliefs. Before Christianity arrived in the eleventh century, the Norse gods of the Vikings and pagan rituals dominated spiritual beliefs and practices in Sweden. The Vikings believed three levels of life existed. The gods existed on the top level, while humans, giants, dwarfs, and dark elves lived on the middle level. The bottom level was the equivalent of hell.

The Sami also have a history of folk beliefs. In earlier times, their beliefs were animistic and shaman-centered. Each village had a shaman, a person who contacted the gods and gave the villagers advice. The use of the shaman continued until the 1940s. The Sami believe all objects have a soul and every force of nature is controlled by a god. Consequently, the Sami try to move around quietly in the wilderness, and excessive noise is discouraged.

NORSE GODS

A number of Norse gods are still familiar to us today, such as Odin, god of wisdom and war. Other Norse gods include Thor, the god of thunder; Frey, god of fertility; and Berserker, a warrior whose frenzy in battle transformed him into a howling wolf or a bear. The English word *berserk*, meaning "to go crazy," is derived from this god's name.

Below: The interior of many Swedish churches is defined by high, arched ceilings.

Language and Literature

The official language of Sweden is Swedish. Swedish is related to the Norwegian, Danish, and Icelandic languages, all of which are a subgroup of the Germanic languages. The Swedish language has been influenced largely by German but also draws some words from English and French. The Swedish Sami generally speak North Sami, or North Lapp, and the country also has a small minority group of Finnish speakers.

Information about early Swedish language has been gathered from runic inscriptions from between A.D. 600 and 1225. Changes in the language began to take place in the fourteenth and fifteenth centuries. The birth of modern Swedish is generally considered to have occurred in 1526, with the translation of the New Testament into Swedish. A standard language soon began to emerge, with the main dialects of Stockholm and Lake Mälaren as its model. In 1836, a Swedish grammar handbook was published by the Swedish Academy, and a dictionary soon followed.

Swedish has a tone, or pitch, accent and has been described by many English speakers as having a singsong rhythm. Swedish also has two noun genders (neuter and common), and the definite article is placed after the noun.

Above: **Hand-painted letter boxes adorned with a family's name are a common sight throughout Sweden.**

Below: **The modern Swedish language, as shown in this sign, took centuries to evolve into its present-day form.**

Left: Selma Lagerlöf (*far left*) and Astrid Lindgren (*left*) are two of Sweden's most famous women authors. Their different styles of writing have captured audiences both within Sweden and beyond.

Literature

Sweden is rich in literary tradition and began producing literature as early as the Middle Ages. The oldest existing manuscript is the *Västgötalagan* (vest-yoo-TAH-lah-gen), or Law of West Gotland, a legal code written in 1220. The translation of the Bible into Swedish in 1541 was probably one of the most important literary events in Sweden. Not only did it initiate modern Swedish, but it also provided an inexhaustible source for poets in later years.

Twentieth-century literature was revolutionized by August Strindberg (1891–1974). He wrote novels, plays, short stories, and poems that were usually critical of society. Today, Strindberg is regarded as Sweden's greatest author.

The early twentieth century saw the emergence of another popular writer, Selma Lagerlöf (1858–1940). Lagerlöf wrote novels about country life in her home county of Värmland. Although her works were based on Sweden, they had an international appeal. She was the first woman and Swede to be awarded the Nobel Prize for Literature in 1909. Since then, six other Swedish writers have won the prize.

One of today's best-known Swedish authors is Astrid Lindgren (1907–), author of the *Pippi Longstocking* books. Her books mix fantasy with reality and feature mischievous characters that appeal to children. She has won many prestigious awards, including the Swedish Academy's Gold Medal in 1971 and the International Book Award in 1993.

ALFRED NOBEL: FATHER OF THE NOBEL PRIZE

Every year on December 10, the prestigious Nobel Prizes are awarded. The prizes are the legacy of Swedish inventor and industrialist Alfred Nobel and reflect his passionate interest in chemistry, physics, medicine, literature, and peace.
(A Closer Look, page 54)

Arts

Provincial folk art and traditional crafts have had a huge impact on the development of Swedish arts. Over the centuries, however, artists have also been influenced by ideas and trends brought back by Swedish traders. Today, Swedes appreciate a wide variety of arts, and the country has made major contributions to the art, architecture, design, music, and film industries.

Above: **Many of Carl Milles's monumental sculptures, such as this one entitled** *Europa and the Bull*, **are housed at the Millesgården, located in Stockholm.**

Painters and Sculptors

Sweden has produced many fine painters of international renown. Anders Zorn (1860–1920) is well known for his paintings of nudes and his realistic depictions of scenes of rural Swedish customs. One of his famous paintings is *Midsummer Dance* (1897), which portrays the traditional dancing that takes place during Midsummer's Eve festivities. Carl Larsson (1853–1919) painted moving portraits of his home and family in watercolors that established his reputation both in Sweden and overseas.

Sweden has also produced some prominent sculptors. In the early twentieth century, Carl Milles (1875–1955) became the country's best-known sculptor, mainly for his monuments and sculpture fountains.

THE ICE HOTEL

Each year, on the shores of the Torne River in northern Sweden, a famous ice hotel is designed and created from thousands of tons (metric tonnes) of chiseled ice and snow.
(A Closer Look, page 52)

Music

Franz Berwald (1796–1868) is regarded as Sweden's most important nineteenth-century composer. He was the founder of musical romanticism in Sweden and made a great impact on the development of the Swedish symphony. His works blended romantic and classical styles and portrayed an original use of harmony. Swedes enjoy the music of symphony and chamber orchestras, as well as more modern types of music, such as jazz and pop. Traditional folk music also occupies a place in the heart of many Swedes.

Architecture and Design

For centuries, the blending of structures with the surrounding scenery has been an important feature of Swedish architecture, and all Swedish buildings, from manor houses to sixteenth-century castles, reflect this principle. Today, Swedish architecture emphasizes buildings that are simple in design and let in the maximum amount of natural light. Among Sweden's most distinguished architects is Ragnar Östberg (1866–1945), who designed the Stockholm City Hall.

Like architecture, Swedish design stresses simplicity and functionality. In the early 1930s, Sweden became a stronghold for the functionalist movement, an artistic movement that promoted usefulness above appearance.

SWEDISH POP MUSIC

Sweden's own style of pop music entered the world music scene in the early 1970s with the pop phenomenon ABBA. Since then, many Swedish bands have enjoyed international success.
(A Closer Look, page 62)

SKANSEN

Swedish architectural styles and buildings have been memorialized at Skansen, an open-air historical museum located in Stockholm. Traditional buildings from all over the country are on display here to show visitors how people lived before Sweden became industrialized. Exhibits include farmhouses, churches, and furniture.

Left: Founded by Ingvar Kamprad (*left*) in 1943, IKEA, the Swedish home interior giant, sells functional and practical products at reasonable prices. This style of home interiors and household items is a perfect example of "Swedish modern," which emphasizes function.

Left: Located in Stockholm, the baroque-style Operan, or Royal Opera House, houses the Royal Swedish Opera.

Performing Arts

Theater, opera, and dance thrive in Sweden. Swedish theater is predominantly international, and many foreign plays are performed every year. Established in 1788, the Royal Dramatic Theater in Stockholm is Sweden's leading theater. Modern theater is also well represented by companies such as Folkoperan, which performs contemporary plays dealing with pressing social issues.

Sweden also has many fine opera houses, in which audiences can enjoy classical as well as modern operas. At certain times of the year, the opera houses stage open-air concerts with music by international composers, such as Wilhelm Richard Wagner and Richard Strauss.

For many years, ballet was the most popular form of dance in Sweden. In recent years, however, Sweden's appreciation has expanded to include many types of international dance, such as square dancing and flamenco. Sweden's own form of historic folk dancing has also experienced a comeback.

The Swedish Film Industry

In 1963, the Swedish Film Institute was established to promote the Swedish film industry. Although most Swedish movies are shown only in Sweden, some have been international box office hits, such as some of the works of directors Ingmar Bergman and Lasse Hallström. Well-known Swedish actors and actresses include Max von Sydow, Greta Garbo, and Ingrid Bergman.

MOVING THEATERS

Many theater companies travel around the country, presenting thousands of performances a year. One such group is the English Theater Company, a Swedish company that performs plays only in English, such as adaptations of *The Canterbury Tales* (c. 1387) or *A Christmas Carol* (1843).

INGMAR BERGMAN: HIS LIFE AND WORK

Swedish film director Ingmar Bergman (1918–) is known internationally for his films and has gained critical acclaim around the world. He has been hailed as one of the major filmmakers of all time.
(A Closer Look, page 46)

Handicrafts

Swedish craftwork is well known for its high quality. Swedes have produced handmade objects, mainly made from wood, since the early-nineteenth century. The most famous Swedish wood carvings are *Dalahäst* (DAH-lah-hest), or Dala horses. Made in the county of Dalarna, these brightly painted wooden horses have evolved into a symbol of all Swedish handicrafts. Glassmaking is another highly reputable craft that continues to adapt and change with the times. Other famous crafts in Sweden include ceramics, silver, and textiles. Swedes have received global recognition for the simple beauty and functional design of all these crafts.

Museums

Sweden's cultural institutions, including its museums, are largely maintained through state funding. The best-known museum is the National Museum in Stockholm, which houses Sweden's main art collection. Other museums include the Vasa Museum and the Swedish Museum of Natural History. Private academic societies, such as the Royal Swedish Academy, also contribute to the promotion of the arts.

GLASSMAKING AND THE KINGDOM OF CRYSTAL

Located in the southeastern part of the Småland Highlands, the Kingdom of Crystal is famous for its variety of glassworks that combines ancient glassmaking techniques with modern art.
(*A Closer Look*, page 48)

Below: This woman is sanding Dala horses in a workshop in Dalarna.

Leisure and Festivals

Virtually all Swedish leisure and recreation activities center around enjoying the great outdoors. Swedes like to get away from city life as often as possible, and many spend their vacations or weekends in the countryside. Many Swedes own or have access to a summer house, and about 600,000 of these homes are located in the country's rural areas, especially on the islands around Stockholm.

Walking is a favorite pastime, and families often go for walks on weekends. The country has a network of walking paths, many of which have rest stations. At over 300 miles (483 km) in length, the Kungsleden, or Royal Route, is the most well-known trail.

Hunting and fishing are also favorite outdoor activities. Deer, elk, and foxes are plentiful in the country's forests. Game fish include pike, salmon, and trout. When rivers freeze, people cut holes in the ice and drop their fishing lines through them. Cycling and hot air ballooning are also popular.

Below: Swedes often combine cycling with a peaceful picnic in one of the country's parks and gardens, such as Djurgården in Stockholm.

Allemansrätten

The enjoyment of nature is so important to Swedes that the government has passed a law known as *Allemansrätten* (AH-leh-manz-reh-ten), or the Right of Public Access. Although many nations enforce rights of public access, Sweden's law is the most all-encompassing in the world. The law allows anyone to use any forest or field and includes walking; picking wildflowers, berries, or mushrooms; or even camping on private property.

Other Pastimes

Sweden has several aquariums, butterfly houses, birdhouses, and zoos that are enjoyed by natives and tourists alike. Swedes enjoy attending the theater or going to museums and galleries to see exhibitions. Sweden is also a nation of readers. About 65 million books are borrowed from the country's public libraries every year.

Swedes enjoy a challenging game of chess, and several chess clubs and societies are scattered throughout the country. Swedes also like to meet with friends to chat and drink coffee in sidewalk cafés.

Above: **A Swedish family in central Sweden enjoys a peaceful ride through the countryside on a more traditional form of transportation.**

SAFARI

A popular summer trip for Swedish families is a safari, or a trip through a large wildlife preserve. A safari allows everyone to see the animals living in their natural habitats.

Sports

Sports are extremely popular in Sweden. The country's varied landscape and climates are perfect for almost any type of sport.

Swedes have access to an abundance of snow and ice during winter, and the nation is known for its winter sports and facilities. Skiing, in particular, has developed rapidly over the past few decades. Downhill ski areas are common throughout the central and northern parts of the country, and cross-country skiing is also popular.

Swedes are avid fans of both ice hockey and bandy, another sport played on ice. Similar to ice hockey, bandy is played almost exclusively in Scandinavia. A team consists of eight to eleven players who wear skates and use curved sticks to hit a ball. The

SKIING: A NATIONAL PASTIME

Thousands of Swedes put on their skis every year to enjoy the winter sport of skiing, probably the country's favorite cold-weather activity.
(*A Closer Look, page 58*)

Left: **Swedish tennis player Stefan Edberg played against and defeated German Boris Becker in the 1990 Wimbledon, or All-England, Championships. Following his victory at Wimbledon, Edberg was ranked the number one player in the world in 1990. He retired from the sport in 1996.**

use of a ball instead of a puck makes bandy an even faster sport than ice hockey.

Summer sports include golf, and Sweden is home to over 360 golf courses. Soccer is also a popular sport and has a huge following. The country has many local and regional teams, all of which are ranked in the country's different leagues and divisions. The country's national team won third place in the World Cup Championships in 1994, coming behind Brazil and Italy, respectively.

Tennis ranks as another popular summer sport in Sweden, and many children learn how to play this game at a very early age. Internationally known players, such as Björn Bjorg, Stefan Edberg, and Mats Wilander, have helped promote the sport.

Below: **The Stockholm Marathon is held annually in June. Both men and women compete in the marathon, which is one of the largest in the world.**

Sweden excels at badminton and was the host of the first official World Championship in Badminton in 1977. The Swedish team won the championship's mixed doubles in 1985 and 1993. Sweden also won an impressive twelve world champion titles in table tennis.

Orienteering is also increasing in popularity. Orienteering is similar to cross-country running; participants run a course as fast as possible, following the route on a map and passing certain points marked along the route. This sport now attracts over 100,000 runners. The largest orienteering events in Sweden are Fernagars and O-ringen.

SYDNEY 2000

Swedish athletes took home four gold medals, five silver medals, and three bronze medals from the Olympic Games held in Sydney, Australia, in September 2000.

Festivals

The Swedish population celebrates many secular and religious festivals throughout the year.

After a long, cold winter in most parts of the country, Swedes celebrate the coming of spring every year on April 30 with songs and bonfires. This festival is known as Valborgsmassoafton, or Walpurgis Night, and dates back to the Viking era.

Easter is an important religious celebration. The festival begins with Palm Sunday. As palms cannot grow in Sweden's cold climate, many Swedes decorate twigs with colored feathers and place the twigs in water so that they sprout new leaves in time for the holiday. On Easter Sunday, families go to church and then return home to eat a large meal together. Also at Easter, young boys and girls dress as Easter witches and visit their neighbors, from whom they receive small gifts.

Another popular festival in Sweden is Midsummer's Eve. The festival was originally celebrated to encourage a good harvest in autumn. Today, it is a national holiday that takes place on the Friday closest to June 24. Families and friends gather to eat herring and fresh potatoes.

Below: **Swedes of all ages join in the Midsummer's Eve festivities in Sundborn, the village where the artist Carl Larsson and his wife, Karin, lived.**

Above: **Santa Claus and his reindeer visit Sami children in Swedish Lapland.**

Saint Lucia's Day occurs on December 13. This modern-day festival includes a young girl dressed all in white with a crown of candles on her head. Girl attendants, similarly dressed, follow her in a procession. Boys, called star-boys, also participate in the ceremony. The group of girls and boys visits places such as schools, hospitals, and churches; sings songs; and brings *Lussekatter* (LOOSE-cah-ter), or "Lucia's cats," a type of sweet, saffron bun. This ceremony represents the hope of the returning sun in the midst of the dark Swedish winter.

The most important religious holiday in Sweden is Christmas. The Swedish people prepare for Christmas with Advent, a four-week period preceding Christmas. During this time, a candle is lit every Sunday in a special Advent candlestick. When all four candles in the candlestick are burning, Christmas is ready to begin. Families decorate their homes and bake special treats. On Christmas Eve, Swedish children eagerly await Santa Claus, who personally hands out gifts to everyone. On Christmas Day, many Swedes get up early to attend *julottan* (YULE-ooh-tan), a special church service that takes place at 6:00 or 7:00 a.m.

The Swedish flag is honored on June 6. On this day, all cities and towns fly flags, and the monarch presents the national flag to Swedish organizations and societies at a special ceremony.

Food

Sweden's diverse natural surroundings and climate are reflected in the diversity of its cuisine. Although Swedish food is generally simple, consisting mainly of fish and potato dishes with cheese and fruits to complement them, the traditional Swedish table has a lot to offer.

Swedes love fish, especially salmon, that has been smoked, marinated, or cured with dill and salt. They also enjoy *lutfisk* (LOOT-fisk), or cod soaked in lye. After the fish has been seasoned properly, it is sautéed in a pan with butter, salt, and pepper. Lutfisk is a traditional Christmas dish. Another popular fish dish is *surströmming* (SOOR-strom-ing), or fermented Baltic herring. Surströmming is considered an acquired taste and has a strong odor. This odor is the result of the fermentation process that uses just enough salt to stop the fish from spoiling. Surströmming is usually served with boiled potatoes and onions and is often rolled into a slice of thin, flat, unleavened bread.

Above: **The Veranden Restaurant is one of the many fine restaurants Swedes frequent in Stockholm, the country's capital.**

Crayfish parties are popular in August. At these parties, huge amounts of crayfish are boiled with dill, sugar, and salt, and then eaten by hand.

The Swedes also have a sweet tooth. A popular dessert is *ostkaka* (oost-KAK-ah), or cheesecake. Ostkaka is made with fresh milk that has been curdled with rennet. After the cake is baked, it is often topped with fresh fruits or jam. Another sweet treat is Lussekatter. These buns are made by mixing bread dough with saffron. The dough is then shaped into a cross, and raisins are added. The buns are served with coffee on the morning of Saint Lucia's Day.

Sweden ranks second in the world when it comes to drinking coffee. Coffee is usually consumed at breakfast, after lunch, and throughout the day during coffee breaks. Swedes even have special coffee parties called *kafferep* (CAF-ah-rep). Beer and schnapps, or aquavit, are also popular beverages.

SMÖRGÅSBORD

S*mörgåsbord* (smore-gose-BORD) originated in Sweden and offers many different dishes that are meant to be eaten in a specific order. Smörgåsbord was traditionally served on Midsummer's Eve, but today, Swedes enjoy the buffet throughout the year.
(*A Closer Look, page 60*)

COOKING THROUGH THE AGES

The Vikings brought home raw produce, seasonings, and spices from their journeys abroad, while medieval monks brought their knowledge of gardening and growing fruit. In the eighteenth century, cooking techniques such as braising and sautéing were added to the slow-cooking and roasting methods used for centuries by Swedes.

Left: Crayfish is a Swedish delicacy that is in season from the end of July to the beginning of September.

A CLOSER LOOK
AT SWEDEN

Sweden is a country dedicated to efficiency. Even its early inhabitants, such as the Vikings, were expert seafarers and explorers who also successfully created well-run home environments. Today's Swedes share the same love as their forefathers for making the most of what they have been given.

Sweden contains some of the most beautiful countryside in the world. The land is home to a wide variety of wildlife, including the mysterious, threatened wolverine. The cold

Opposite: **The King's Garden in Stockholm's city center is a popular place for Swedes to relax and spend their free time.**

weather of northern and central Sweden provides the perfect environment for Swedes to pursue their beloved sport of skiing, as well as build the world-famous Ice Hotel. Sweden also has an impressive cultural tradition. From filmmaker Ingmar Bergman to the fine glass and crystal of the Kingdom of Crystal, Swedes have good reason to be proud of their cultural accomplishments.

Whether addressing critical environmental issues, such as acid rain, or restoring historical treasures, such as the ancient warship *Vasa*, one thing is clear — Sweden is a country with a rich heritage and a history of excellence.

Above: **The simple wooden houses in the county of Dalarna blend in perfectly with the countryside.**

Acid Rain

Acid rain has been a major cause for concern in Sweden for the past forty years. Acid rain is caused by emissions of sulfur dioxide and nitrogen oxides into the atmosphere. These gases then combine with the water vapor in clouds. When rain falls, it is very acidic and results in the acidification of lakes, other water sources, and soils, as well as damage to structures and monuments.

Reports of large amounts of dead fish in the lakes of western Sweden in the 1960s were the first indication that acid rain had become a major problem. Today, about 10,000 Swedish lakes are so acidified that many organisms cannot survive in them.

Soils, especially forest soils, have also been adversely affected by acid rain. Since Scandinavian soil generally lacks limestone,

BUILDING CORROSION

Many of Sweden's historical monuments, such as the prehistoric rock carvings at the Tanum Museum of Rock Carvings, are slowly being corroded by acid rain and airborne acidic substances. In an attempt to combat this corrosion, museum officials have erected a canopy over the rocks to protect them.

the soil is more vulnerable to the process of acidification than soil in other European countries. Acid rain causes minerals in the soil to weather slowly, reducing the soil's fertility. Since acidification weakens soil chemistry processes, tree growth, vegetation, and groundwater are all affected. If allowed to continue, acid rain will seriously damage forest vegetation and animal life.

The main cause of acid rain in Sweden is the burning of oil and coal, which leads to sulfur dioxide deposition in the atmosphere. In addition, more than half the nitrogen oxides comes from traffic exhaust fumes, while the rest comes mostly from combustion plants located both in Sweden and in surrounding countries.

Above: In an attempt to revive animal and plant life in Sweden's acidified waters, about 200,000 tons (181,440 m tonnes) of limestone are spread over the country's lakes, such as this one in western Sweden. As the limestone dissolves, the water becomes less acidic. This liming program is the largest in the world; more than seven thousand lakes have been limed since the 1970s.

Since the late 1960s, Sweden has worked diligently to reduce acid rain and its effects. The country banned the burning of high-sulfur oils in 1969. This was followed by a series of measures that led to a fall in sulfur dioxide emissions from 992,063 tons (900,000 m tonnes) in 1970 to 76,058 tons (69,000 m tonnes) in 1997. Methods used included decreasing the use of oil and increasing the use of nuclear energy, which in turn reduces the need to use fossil fuels. In 1991, a tax was imposed on all combustion plants for every ton (0.9072 m tonne) of nitrogen oxides emitted. This measure also helped reduce acid rain drastically.

While Swedish soil and water is expected to continue acidifying in the immediate future, the process has, at least, been significantly reduced. Both the government and the Swedish population take acid rain seriously and continue to battle the problem to secure the beauty of Sweden for future generations.

Above: **This scientist skims the surface of one of Sweden's acidified lakes to see how much deposition has occurred in the lake.**

Left: **Exhaust fumes from Sweden's constant flow of traffic contribute to increased levels of nitrogen oxides present in the atmosphere.**

A GLOBAL PROBLEM

Acidifying substances travel long distances, so the problem of acid rain knows no boundaries. Although Sweden reduced its sulfur emissions by over 80 percent by 1995, about 90 percent of current acidic deposits come from other countries, primarily the United Kingdom, Germany, and Poland. The Swedish government has made a huge effort to educate the citizens and politicians of surrounding countries about the serious problem of acid rain.

Ingmar Bergman: His Life and Work

Seldom is one person gifted enough to produce art that contains the complexities and turmoil not only of his or her native country but of the entire world. Even rarer is for that person to be celebrated and considered a genius during his or her own lifetime. Yet these accolades are true of Ernst Ingmar Bergman.

Bergman was born on July 14, 1918, in Uppsala. The young Bergman grew up heavily influenced by his parents and the Lutheran Church, of which his father was a pastor. Bergman attended the University of Stockholm, where he studied art, history, and literature. He also became actively involved in the theater, working as both actor and writer.

In 1944, he began working as a director at Hälsingborg municipal theater, where he commissioned an original screenplay *Hets*, or *Frenzy*. Directed by Sweden's then leading film director, Alf Sjöberg, the movie was a success both at home and abroad. In 1945, Bergman wrote and directed his own film *Kris*, or *Crisis*. By then, his career was well underway.

Left (from left to right): **Tomas Hanzon, Liv Ullman, Lena Endre, and Christer Henrikson were present at the Cannes Film Festival 2000 in France to see the premier of their movie** *Trolösa,* **or** *Faithless.* **The movie was based on a script written by Ingmar Bergman.**

From 1946 to 1982, Bergman wrote and/or produced over forty movies. A huge number of these are considered notable and of a high quality — quite an achievement, when taking into account the volume produced.

Bergman's first films dealt mainly with romantic issues, including disillusionment and bad and good relationships. In *Sawdust and Tinsel* (1953), he used relationships within a traveling circus to symbolize human suffering through misplaced love and the ultimate loneliness of the human condition. In 1955, Bergman directed *Sommernattens leende*, or *Smiles of a Summer Night*, a romantic comedy-drama that gained him international fame. He went on to produce *The Seventh Seal* (1956), *Wild Strawberries* (1957), *Through a Glass Darkly* (1962), *Winter Light* (1962), and *The Silence* (1963). In these movies, Bergman moves away from romance toward mortality, sanity, and the presence of evil in the world.

Bergman continued to produce movies until the early 1990s and plans to continue writing as long as possible.

BERGMAN'S ACCOMPLISHMENTS

Bergman's films have a unique style and are of the highest quality, both artistically and professionally. His work introduced many people to the idea of the complete filmmaker — someone who writes and directs an entire piece of work and uses the medium of film to express ideas and perceptions. He gained international fame for Sweden while probing serious questions that haunt everyone. His work is no less intense or moving today than it was forty years ago.

Glassmaking and the Kingdom of Crystal

Glass has the ability to awaken our imagination and enliven our senses. Glass is versatile and sturdy, yet smooth and fragile. Creating glass requires heating fine sand to a certain viscosity and then shaping it. Formulas for glassmaking date back as far as 2000 B.C. Swedes began making glass in the sixteenth century, and, today, they are world famous for their exquisite glass and crystal.

King Gustav I Vasa was Sweden's first glass pioneer. He originally tried to establish a glassworks factory in Stockholm, but large amounts of fuel were needed to heat the glass properly. The best place for such resources was the densely forested Småland Highlands in southeastern Sweden. The glassworks industry set up shop there in 1742, and the Kingdom of Crystal was born.

The Kingdom of Crystal is so called because some twenty glassworks are grouped within a radius of a few dozen miles (km). The styles of these glassworks vary from the most graceful crystal sculpture to sturdy, casual dinnerware.

Two of the most famous glassworks businesses are Kosta and Orrefors. Kosta is the oldest glassworks shop in Sweden and still makes glass by hand. Founded in 1742, Kosta keeps up with the

Above: **A glassblower at Orrefors is molding newly formed glass after heating fine sand in a furnace that reaches a temperature of 2,606° F (1,430° C).**

latest designs and is often called the mother of the Swedish glass industry. Orrefors began as an ironworks factory in 1726 but started making glass in 1898. Although it began its glassmaking days producing jars and inkwells, Orrefors soon took a more artistic turn and began to engrave or etch designs on glassware after hiring Simon Gate and Edward Hald in 1916 and 1917, respectively. Gate and Hald were the first artists to be involved directly in glass design, and their innovative designs won first prize for Orrefors at the Paris International Exhibition of Decorative Arts in 1925. This prestigious prize cemented Orrefors's status as an artistic glass manufacturer.

All the glassworks in the Kingdom of Crystal now employ a number of noted glasswork artists who help keep Sweden and the Kingdom of Crystal on the cutting edge of technology and style. At present, Kosta has the artistic skills of Ann Wåhlström and Göran Wärff, while Orrefors employs Lena Bergström.

All the glassworks in the Kingdom of Crystal are open to the public, and visitors can observe the skilled artists at work. Tourism is a huge industry at the Kingdom of Crystal, which receives over one million visitors each year.

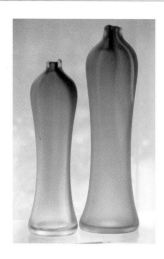

Above: **Swedish glass and crystal are famous worldwide, and half the country's production is exported, mainly to the United States.**

Left: **Orrefors employs talented artists to engrave beautiful designs on its glass and crystal.**

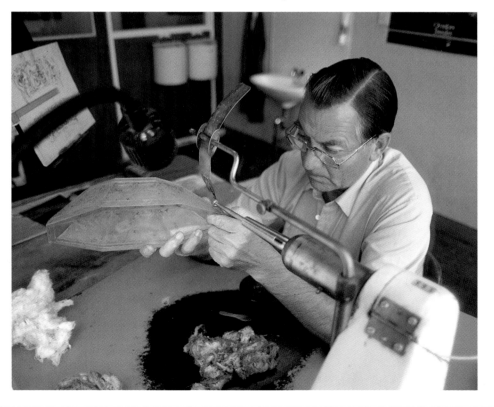

Gustav I Vasa

Gustav I Vasa was king of Sweden from 1523 until his death in 1560. He is credited with establishing Sweden as an independent nation-state and bringing the Reformation to Sweden.

Born in 1496, Gustav was the son of a Swedish senator. During his childhood, Sweden was part of the Kalmar Union that was ruled by Christian II of Denmark. Following the 1517 to 1518 war against Denmark, the young Gustav led a rebellion against the Danes occupying Sweden in 1520. Realizing he needed help, he gained support from the city of Lübeck in Germany, whose merchants felt threatened by Christian's aggressive economic policies. In return, Gustav promised the merchants a monopoly on Sweden's foreign trade. With their

THE STOCKHOLM BLOODBATH

Backed by the pope, the Danish king Christian II invaded Sweden to fight the Swedish anti-Kalmar faction led by Sten Sture the Younger. After defeating Sture's forces and taking Stockholm, Christian II had over eighty Swedish nobles executed for heresy in September 1520. Further executions followed throughout Sweden and Finland. Outrage at the executions spread throughout Sweden and led to the final phase of the Swedish war of secession from the Kalmar Union, under the leadership of Gustav I Vasa.

Left: King Gustav I Vasa gave Sweden nearly forty years of strong, intelligent rule and established the country as a nation in its own right. Gustav was loved by many and hated by many; he was probably Sweden's most influential monarch.

help, Gustav overthrew Christian II and ousted the Danes from Sweden. In doing so, he effectively dissolved the Kalmar Union and paved the way for Sweden to become the independent world power that Gustav envisioned.

Above: **King Gustav I Vasa presided over many ceremonies and met countless statesmen throughout his reign as king of Sweden. By the latter part of his reign, Gustav had developed a strong government administration system that was centered around the crown.**

Elected as king on June 6, 1523, Gustav's early years as king were clouded by troubles. He was a strong ruler who made his own decisions, and many politicians and noblemen did not like this. He also faced economic and religious problems.

As a means to pay his debts to Lübeck and to strengthen royal authority, Gustav imposed heavy taxes and, by doing so, introduced measures that led to the Swedish Reformation. In 1527, the legislature allowed Gustav to confiscate land from the Roman Catholic Church. This appropriation added enormously to the wealth of the state and essentially achieved Gustav's goal for financial stability. Gustav also freed Swedish trade from the monopoly of the Lübeck merchants during the so-called Count's War between claimants to the Danish crown from 1534 to 1536.

Although Gustav was a peaceloving and diplomatic man, a strong army and navy developed during his reign. In addition, in 1544, the legislature declared the monarchy hereditary rather than electoral, ensuring the crown for Vasa generations to come.

The Ice Hotel

In the village of Jukkasjärvi, located in the center of Swedish Lapland, the famous Ice Hotel is built every year on the shores of the Torne River. As soon as the temperature drops to 26° F (-3° C), construction of the hotel begins, using building materials provided by nature.

An amazing 30,000 tons (27,216 m tonnes) of snow is "harvested" and sprayed into specially made metal molds. Once the snow hardens, the molds are removed and used over and over again. An additional 10,000 tons (9,070 m tonnes) of crystal clear ice is taken from the Torne River and used for various structural and furniture needs.

Left: **Everything in the Ice Hotel is made from ice, including the light fixtures and tableware. The main reason it is possible to build the hotel year after year is the unsurpassed cleanliness and purity of the snow and ice in the region of Jukkasjärvi. The Ice Hotel makes a strong case for environmentalists and highlights the benefits of keeping the world clean.**

Covering an area of 37,674 square feet (3,500 square m), the hotel opens in December and stays open until it melts, usually in early May. Depending on the temperature outside and the number of hotel guests, the temperature inside the hotel varies between 25° F and 16° F (-4° C and -9° C). Beds are well-equipped for extreme temperatures, with reindeer skins, a thermal sleeping bag, a sleeping mat, and sheets. The hotel accommodates over one hundred guests, and each room is uniquely designed. In addition to the suites, the hotel includes an ice chapel, an ice art exhibition hall, a movie theater, and the world-famous Absolut Ice Bar.

The stylish Absolut Ice Bar is a perfect meeting place for guests who brave the Ice Hotel. A truly international mix of patrons visits the bar, with tourists from Japan, the United States, England, Germany, Spain, France, and Poland, as well as Swedes.

Below: **After a night's sleep in one of the hotel suites, guests sip a hot drink, then enjoy an early morning sauna.**

Well-chilled drinks can be enjoyed in glasses made entirely of ice. Guests can then move on to enjoy the various ice art collections gathered and displayed throughout the hotel. The ice chapel is a popular location for visitors and locals alike to host a wedding or christening.

The hotel opened the Ice Hotel Art Center in 2000. The center houses ice art, a picture show on a screen of ice, and miniature versions of the ice hotels built in previous years.

The Ice Hotel is fully booked during the last week in January when people come from all over to attend the Kiruna Snow Festival. This week-long festival includes cultural events, such as theater and art exhibitions, as well as dog and reindeer races and a spectacular snow-sculpture competition.

Alfred Nobel: Father of the Nobel Prize

Alfred Nobel was born in Stockholm on October 21, 1833. His father was an engineer and inventor, and his mother came from a wealthy, upper-class family.

After spending most of his early years in Russia, Alfred Nobel began his research in explosives when his father moved the family back to Sweden. Nobel soon became interested in nitroglycerin for practical use in construction work. (Nitroglycerin is a highly explosive liquid that was discovered by Italian chemist Ascanio Sobrero in 1847.) During one of the many explosions that resulted from Nobel's experiments, his youngest brother, Emil, was killed in 1864. Nobel, however, could not abandon his work. Finally, he found a way to stabilize nitroglycerin by mixing it with

Left: Before inventing dynamite, Alfred Nobel was stereotyped as a "mad scientist" because of the number of accidents that occurred during his many experiments.

NOBEL'S CHILDHOOD

At the age of nine, Nobel moved with his family to Russia, where his father had established an armaments factory. The success of the factory soon enabled Nobel's father to give his children an excellent education. By the age of sixteen, Alfred Nobel was fluent in Swedish, Russian, French, English, and German. He especially enjoyed English literature and poetry, as well as chemistry and physics.

silica, shaping it into rods, and inserting it into casings. Naming this invention dynamite, Nobel was granted patents for his discovery in Britain in 1867 and in the United States in 1868.

The market for his invention was huge, and Nobel became very wealthy. Dynamite was soon used worldwide to blast tunnels, cut canals, and build roads and railways. Over the next several years, Nobel founded factories and laboratories in more than twenty countries, including France, Germany, and Scotland.

His passion for inventing did not die, and Nobel continued to work on other inventions, such as artificial silk and leather. By the time of his death in 1896, Nobel had over 350 patents in various countries.

The Nobel Prize

When Nobel died, he left most of his fortune in trust to establish prizes in the areas of physics, chemistry, peace, medicine, and literature. The Nobel Prizes, first awarded in 1901, are given out annually on December 10. Each award consists of a gold medal, a diploma, and a sum of money. With the addition of the Prize for Economic Sciences in Memory of Alfred Nobel, set up by the Bank of Sweden in 1968 and first awarded in 1969, the Nobel Prizes are among the most prestigious awards today.

The Sami

The Sami are some of Scandinavia's earliest settlers. They live in Norway, Finland, and Sweden, with a very small population in Russia. Sweden is home to approximately 20,000 Sami, a number second only to Norway's 30,000 to 40,000. Today, two main groups of Sami reside in the northernmost part of Sweden.

The forest Sami live in the abundant forests of Sweden and mainly fish and hunt for a living. Families usually form small villages close to a river and are semi-nomadic. While this group made up the majority of Swedish Sami in the past, recent expansions and government claims to land have forced many of the forest Sami to give up their way of life. These Sami either go into the cities to look for work or try farming.

The other major group of Sami in Sweden are the reindeer Sami, whose economy depends primarily on reindeer. Although this particular Sami culture is only a few hundred years old, it is

Left: **Villagers and the Sami gather at markets in towns and villages throughout Swedish Lapland to trade products, such as reindeer meat and various types of handicrafts.**

often seen as the typical Sami culture. The importance of reindeer to these Sami is exhibited by the fact that approximately four hundred different words for *reindeer* exist in their language. Due to the continual shrinking of their habitat, many of these Sami now pursue careers outside of raising reindeer. They have industrial jobs in the cities or make crafts, which they try to sell.

The Sami, however, are a proud and resilient people who have not yielded easily to modern setbacks. They have their own flag and consider themselves a separate nation from Sweden. In 1956, the Nordic Sami Council was established, with four members representing the Swedish Sami. In 1993, the Swedish Sami parliament, or *Sametinget* (SAH-may-ting-it) was formed. The responsibilities of the thirty-one elected members are to foster Sami culture, monitor and encourage the use of the Sami language, and advise the Swedish authorities on Sami rights. The Sami also work hard to keep their language and traditions alive, particularly in the area of education, where Sami children can complete their schooling at one of the six state-run Sami schools. Thanks to their perseverance and a general growing awareness of Sami culture, there is good reason to believe the Sami will survive as a group in Sweden for many years to come.

SAMI LITERATURE AND ARTS

Sami folk music has a distinct singing style in which melody and verse are equally important. The lyrics express feelings of sorrow, anger, and love. Today, this type of folk music is witnessing a revival, but the songs are now accompanied by musical instruments. Written Sami literature increased in the early 1980s, but the most famous book written in the Sami language is still Johan Turi's (1854–1936) *Muittalus samid birra*, or *A Story about Lapps*, published in 1910.

Skiing: A National Pastime

In centuries past, the Swedish people used skis primarily for military purposes. Today, however, skiing has become a means of recreation and enjoyment. This winter sport is arguably the most popular in Sweden. Swedish children learn at a very young age how to maneuver on skis, and many Swedes excel at the sport. The country has enjoyed this exhilarating winter sport for a long time, and the people show no signs of abandoning its challenges.

Cross-country skiing is the most popular type of skiing in Sweden. In its noncompetitive form, the sport is called snow touring. Races are held on circular courses, and lengths vary from 3 to 31 miles (5 to 50 km) for both men and women. Two techniques can be used — classical, which keeps the skis parallel with each other at all times; and freestyle, which is more like ice skating and allows for greater speed.

THE VASALOPPET

The Vasaloppet was the vision of newspaper editor Anders Pers, who wanted to commemorate Gustav I Vasa's revolt against King Christian II of Denmark, the ruler of the Kalmar Union. The race was supposed to be an endurance test similar to the journey made by Gustav I Vasa between Mora and Sälen in 1521 to recruit men to fight for Sweden's independence from Denmark.

Left: On November 24, 1999, Swedish skier Fredrick Nyberg produced the fourth best time in the first heat of the men's World Cup giant slalom at Beaver Creek, Colorado.

Sweden is host to the Vasaloppet, the greatest cross-country skiing event in the world. During Vasaloppet week, five different races are held. The most grueling of these races, at an exhausting 56 miles (90 km), is also called the Vasaloppet. The first Vasaloppet event was held on March 19, 1922, with 136 male participants. In 2000, over 40,000 men and women registered in all the races, 15,000 of whom competed in the Vasaloppet race. The Vasaloppet event is watched worldwide, and sixty-nine Swedes have captured the prize during the competition's seventy-six-year history. Even royalty has participated in this prestigious event. In 1977, King Carl XVI Gustaf competed in the Vasaloppet race, finishing with a time of 8 hours, 12 minutes, and 41 seconds.

Sweden is home to over four hundred ski lodges and resorts, further proof of the country's love of skiing. Most of the best areas for skiing are located in central Sweden and extend westward toward Norway's border. Due to Sweden's dark winters, floodlights line most of the trails. March is considered the best time for skiing.

Located in central Sweden, Åre is both Sweden's and northern Europe's largest ski resort. The resort has 44 lifts, 93 supervised trails, and 58 miles (93 km) of cross-country tracks, while the highest point accessible to skiers is 4,180 feet (1,274 m) above sea level.

Above: **Swedes enjoy participating in the many skiing competitions that are held throughout the country.**

A SKIING CHAMPION

Born in 1956, Ingemar Stenmark won an amazing eighty-six World Cup downhill ski races during his sixteen-year career. Forty of these wins were in the slalom event and the other forty-six in the giant slalom event. Stenmark was also the World Cup champion three times from 1976 to 1978 and captured two gold medals at the 1980 Winter Olympics. Few sportsmen have attracted as many Swedish fans as Stenmark did, and whenever he competed in a downhill race, all Sweden stopped to watch.

Smörgåsbord

While Swedish cooking may not be considered as gourmet as other European cuisines, the smörgåsbord is widely considered Sweden's most important contribution to world cuisine. *Smörgåsbord* means "bread and butter table," and it is an integral part of Swedish cuisine.

Historians believe smörgåsbord originated in Sweden at country parties hundreds of years ago, when the guests brought dishes of their own to contribute to the meal. These dishes were laid out on long tables, from which everybody helped themselves. The traditional, huge smörgåsbords began to go out of style in the early 1900s, leaving hosts with the responsibility of preparing all the food themselves. Then, after World War II, the Operakalleren restaurant in Stockholm reintroduced the smörgåsbord. Today, smörgåsbords are commonly considered the favorite way to entertain a large group of people. Restaurants and hotels often serve them as well.

Below: **A smörgåsbord often consists of cold meats, such as liver pâté, smoked reindeer, sliced beef, and ham with vegetable salad.**

Virtually everything imaginable can be found on a smörgåsbord. The complexity and formality, however, varies. A smörgåsbord may be a simple appetizer table, offering bread, butter, cheese, and pickled herring. The meal can also be an elaborate variety of hot and cold dishes, with different kinds of herring; pâtés; cold meats; salads; marinated salmon; *köttbullar* (shot-BULL-ar), or meatballs; and *Janssons frestelse* (YAHN-sons FRES-tel-seh), or Jansson's temptation, a layered potato dish with onions and cream and topped with anchovies.

Whatever the scale of the smörgåsbord, people must follow specific procedures. Traditional etiquette is to begin with the herring, shrimp, and smoked fish, then move on to the salads and cold meats. Next, guests help themselves to the hot dishes, followed by the desserts, often ice cream with cloudberry sauce, which is similar to raspberry sauce. Cheese is the last course of a smörgåsbord. A clean plate is required for each serving. Swedish hosts do not like to see their guests with various selections placed on one plate and consumed at the same time.

Above: **Many hotels provide elaborate smörgåsbords. These delicious buffets are a popular attraction for tourists.**

Swedish Pop Music

Sweden's influence on pop music began in the 1970s, and the country has continued to contribute a great deal to the style and sound of popular artists around the world.

The country's unique sound of music entered the world scene in 1974, with the success of ABBA in the 1974 Eurovision Song Contest, held in Brighton, England. The group's winning song, "Waterloo," was the first of many international hits.

The world enjoyed songs from ABBA throughout the 1970s and early 1980s, with hits including "SOS," "Dancing Queen," and "Fernando." Having a distinct Swedish sound, with modern synthesizers and disco beats adding a contemporary flair, ABBA's music has been described as the perfect pop-Euro-disco balance. The female singers, Agnetha Fältskog and Anni-Frid Lyngstad, were divas long before that word came to be associated with female singers, and they influenced others with their attitudes

Below (from left to right): **Benny Andersson, Anni-Frid Lyngstad, Agnetha Fältskog, and Björn Ulvaeus formed ABBA in 1972. Taking its name from the first initial of each group member, the group was well known in Sweden before it gained international fame.**

and style. ABBA disbanded in 1982, but interest in the band was rekindled in the 1990s, as imitation groups emerged and paid homage to this Swedish pop phenomenon.

Swedish bands that have enjoyed worldwide popularity and success more recently are Ace of Base, Roxette, and The Cardigans. Ace of Base has often been compared to ABBA. Like ABBA, the group consists of two men and two women, and their music has a similar sound, minus the heavy disco influence that ABBA exhibited. Ace of Base's synthesized dance beats were most popular during the early 1990s, with songs like "All That She Wants" and "The Sign" topping the charts. Another Swedish band popular around the same time was the duo Roxette. Musicians Per Gessle and Marie Fredriksson of Roxette created a sharper, edgier sound, and fans worldwide bought millions of their albums. While several of Roxette's albums enjoyed extended popularity in Europe and North America, the single "It Must Have Been Love" from the U.S. box office hit *Pretty Woman* was by far their most successful song. Most recently, the global pop scene has enjoyed the music of The Cardigans, a band formed in Stockholm in 1992. Their single "Love Fool" became a huge hit internationally.

MAMMA MIA!

A box office hit on both sides of the Atlantic, the musical *Mamma Mia!* weaves twenty-two ABBA songs into a story about family and friendship set on a mythical Greek island. ABBA members Björn Ulvaeus and Benny Andersson were actively involved in the production of the musical. *Mamma Mia!* was an instant success in London and took North America by storm in 2000.

The Swedish Welfare State

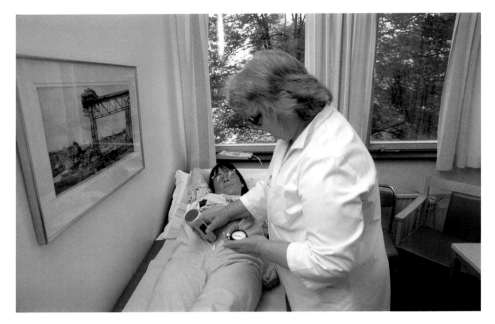

The Swedish welfare state is based on the idea that everyone is entitled to health care, family services, old-age pensions, and other social benefits, regardless of income. All Swedes are entitled to these benefits, and they must pay for them through taxes. Many experts believe Sweden's welfare system is the ideal form of welfare state, and the Swedish model was admired and emulated by other countries for most of the twentieth century. Recent economic problems, however, have threatened the stability of the system.

A Welfare State Is Born

The creation of Sweden's welfare state began in the 1930s, when the Swedish government began to set up a comprehensive welfare plan to cover every conceivable social problem. First, free pre- and postnatal care for mothers and free medical care for children under one year were established. After World War II, the system was expanded and included free school lunches and a system of financial assistance for students. Housing subsidies and child subsidies were increased, and an annual vacation was

THE PEOPLE'S HOME

Coined by Swedish prime minister P. A. Hansson, the "people's home," or the Swedish welfare state, aimed to make Sweden a country in which its citizens would be treated like members of a family, and a sense of equality, cooperation, and security would prevail. The program was established when the Swedish government realized that something had to be done to eliminate the country's high unemployment rate (40 percent) and the falling birth rate following the Great Depression.

implemented. A universal health insurance program, in which everyone received medical care, and a supplementary pension plan were also added.

Benefits and Burdens

Sweden's model worked wonderfully until the early 1980s. The unemployment rate had dropped from 40 percent to 2 percent. The economy boomed, and the population was happier and healthier than it had been for many years.

In the 1980s, however, the system began to falter. The unemployment rate rose sharply, and inflation began to trouble the economy. Taxes were extremely high, and their distribution seemed increasingly unequal. By 1993, some economists were predicting a complete collapse of the welfare system, while others went so far as to say that the model had failed.

The problem was not so much the model but the way in which it was implemented. The government realized its shortcomings and managed to improve the system in the last years of the twentieth century.

THE PROBLEMS WITH THE SWEDISH MODEL

As unemployment, inflation, and the government's budget deficit grew in the early 1980s, many workers complained about having to pay for such an expensive welfare system. Consequently, certain benefits and taxes were cut. When these measures failed, the government introduced a program of spending cuts and tax increases to reduce the deficit. By 1997, both unemployment and the deficit had been reduced, and the government announced the restoration, and even expansion, of some social welfare benefits.

Swedish Women

For hundreds of years, Swedish women had no rights or voice in the political, social, and economic arenas. They could not own property, vote, serve as government representatives, or be employed in the same jobs as men. Over the last two hundred years, however, Swedish women have struggled to win these and other rights.

Traditionally, women had been expected to stay at home, but the women's rights movement in Sweden slowly gained momentum. Their cause was further enhanced toward the end of the 1960s, when economists estimated that if all Swedish women of a working age were to enter the workforce, Sweden's gross national product would increase as much as 30 percent. This growth was appealing to all Swedes, and more and more women began to work. In 1979, the Equal Opportunities Act was passed, which abolished separate male and female wage scales. Before then, women knowingly worked for lower wages than their male counterparts.

HM QUEEN SILVIA

Above: **Queen Silvia of Sweden attended the Women's International Forum at the U.N. headquarters in New York in October 2000.**

Today, women work in all sectors, with the exception of the armed forces. Many Swedish women have taken the lead as local entrepreneurs and have created jobs and income or created new services in their communities. They have also started many small businesses, ranging from day-care centers to car repair shops.

Women are also well-represented in government. Today, at 43 percent, the Riksdag has the highest number of women members of all the parliaments in the world, and the current speaker of the Riksdag is Birg Dahl.

Swedish women have made great progress, but many feel the struggle is far from over. Organizations and women's groups meet regularly throughout Sweden to talk about empowerment and present-day issues, such as gender equality and the need for more funding for and research on women's health concerns. In addition, the Swedish welfare state has suffered in recent years, and this, in turn, has affected single mothers, who now have fewer programs and aid available to them. As times change, so do the issues, and the women of Sweden will undoubtedly continue to make their voices heard.

Above: **Today, more Swedish women are securing jobs in the medical profession, working as research assistants, doctors, or nurses.**

Opposite: **Crown Princess Victoria of Sweden inaugurated the new buildings of a school for physically and mentally disabled children located on the outskirts of Stockholm on December 5, 2000. Women in the Swedish royal family are actively involved in many community projects and charities.**

The Vikings

From the ninth to the eleventh centuries, Vikings from Scandinavia raided and colonized wide areas of Europe. The term *Viking* is believed to have originated from the Swedish word *vik* (vyke), meaning "bay." Vikings are often thought of only as wild and cruel barbarians, but they were also shrewd traders, excellent navigators, and ingenious craftsmen and shipbuilders.

The Vikings lived in large family groups, with up to three generations living under one roof. The women were expected to take care of the home and ensure an ample supply of food throughout the long, dark winters. Women had a fair degree of independence since they managed the farms when their husbands went hunting or trading. Women also exhibited a considerable amount of authority and kept all the household food in chests, the keys to which they alone carried.

The success of boat travel was well known by the Vikings. They are credited with much of the exploring and settling that took place throughout Europe and the North Atlantic during their years of prosperity. The Vikings used two main types of ships for traveling — the longship and the Knórr. The longship was a warship. Ranging from 45 to 75 feet (14 to 23 m), the longship was narrow and had a single square sail. These attributes gave the ship speed and maneuverability, both on the high seas and in rivers. The Vikings did not need harbors to land the longship; it was designed to beach on any type of land. In contrast, the Knórr was a sturdy cargo ship, designed to carry large amounts of men, animals, and supplies. Viking tradesmen generally sailed during the day and landed on a beach at nightfall to eat, sleep, and prepare for another full day of sailing.

The Vikings followed a very specific system of laws. They even had a legislative assembly and a court. Criminals stood trial in front of the court. The facts were presented, and a jury of twelve, twenty-four, or thirty-six people decided whether the person was innocent or guilty.

The Vikings were originally pagans and worshiped a multitude of gods, including Odin, Thor, and Frey. Many Vikings converted to Christianity in the tenth century and are credited with helping spread Christianity throughout Sweden.

Above: **Today, Viking reenactments and festivals are common throughout Sweden.**

EXPLOITS ABROAD

At their peak, Swedish Vikings set up trading posts in what is now eastern Russia and the Ukraine. From there, they controlled the trade routes along the Dnieper River to the Black Sea and Constantinople, as well as to the Caspian Sea. The Vikings also controlled trade across the Baltic Sea.

Opposite: **Regarded by many people as wild barbarians from the north, the Vikings were famous for their ruthless and daring attacks overseas. During these raids, the Vikings destroyed all property that could not be taken with them. They were fierce and powerful warriors.**

The Warship *Vasa*

In the early seventeenth century, Sweden was determined to build an empire around the Baltic Sea. The country was still at war with Poland during the 1620s, thus a powerful navy was paramount. King Gustav II Adolf ordered new warships, and work on the *Vasa* began in 1625.

The *Vasa* was designed to be the mightiest warship in the world, striking fear into the hearts of the Poles and enemies everywhere. Most warships of the time had only one gun deck, but the *Vasa* had two, containing sixty-four heavy artillery cannons and guns. The warship was also equipped to hold three hundred soldiers, ensuring that enough crew members were available to capture an enemy ship once it was downed.

The *Vasa* was ready to sail out of Stockholm harbor on August 10, 1628. Crowds of people gathered to watch the ship's maiden voyage. At the request of King Gustav, many foreign diplomats were also present, as the *Vasa* was meant as a statement of Sweden's naval power for all to see. The *Vasa* set sail and fired a salute. Within minutes, however, a gust of wind hit the *Vasa*, causing the warship to heel to one side. The warship righted itself, only to be blown sideways again. Then, while hundreds watched in horror, the *Vasa* did the last thing anyone expected — it sank.

AT WAR WITH POLAND

The war against Poland had begun before Gustav II Adolf's reign. In 1599, Charles IX seized the Swedish throne, dethroning his nephew Sigismund III Vasa, who was also the king of Poland. This move prompted a dynastic quarrel between Sweden and Poland that lasted for thirty years. Therefore, when Gustav II Adolf became king of Sweden in 1611, he faced the constant threat of a Polish invasion. The continual fighting between the two nations ended in 1629, with the Truce of Altmark in which Sigismund renounced his claim to the Swedish throne.

Of the 150 people on board, between thirty and fifty crew members perished in the disaster. An inquest was set up immediately to determine what had happened. For a time, blame fluctuated between the shipbuilder and the captain, but blame was finally placed on insufficient theoretical knowledge.

No more was heard about the *Vasa* for more than three hundred years. Then, in 1961, the warship was raised from her resting place beneath 100 feet (30 m) of water. Sweden stood still as the seventeenth-century warship surfaced from its watery grave. Archaeologists immediately began preserving and restoring the *Vasa*, and a makeshift Vasa museum was opened soon after the warship had been raised. The official Vasa Museum in Stockholm was inaugurated in 1990.

Today, the Vasa Museum receives nearly 800,000 visitors and earns close to U.S. $5 million a year. The modern building is crowned by three masts and is complete with replicated captain's quarters and a cannon deck. The ship itself is the main attraction. Preserved artifacts, such as watches, games, shoes, and carpenters' tools, provide a look into what seafaring life was like in the seventeenth century.

WHY DID THE *VASA* SINK?

The heavier guns on the *Vasa* had been placed on the upper deck rather than the lower deck, making the warship unstable. The ballast was too light to counterbalance the immense weight of the warship's guns, causing the dramatic heeling of the vessel. The inquest established that the gun ports had been open. Water rushed through the ports when the warship heeled and caused it to sink.

The Wolverine

The wolverine has long fascinated hunters, trappers, and animal lovers. The animal had earned its place in Sami folklore long before other hunters and gatherers began to tell tales of a beast of great cunning, ferocity, and strength. Even today, characters such as Wolverine, the comic book hero from *X-Men*, exemplify the mystery and fascination that surrounds this ferocious animal.

Northwestern Sweden, which is cold and heavily forested, provides the ideal habitat for this animal. While Sweden's population of wolverines used to be significant, the animals are now under serious threat of extinction. Today, only between 150 and 320 wolverines reside in Sweden's northwestern, mountainous regions.

The wolverine is a member of the weasel family. It is usually between 26 and 36 inches (66 to 91 centimeters) long, excluding the long, bushy tail, and weighs from 20 to 66 pounds

Left: **The wolverine is a cross between a weasel and a grizzly bear.**

(9 to 30 kilograms). The wolverine has extremely long, sharp claws and strong teeth. It is always on the move and has large, furry feet that act as snowshoes and help it move quickly. The wolverine usually hunts by ambushing its prey. It generally climbs to the top of a rock or large stump and jumps squarely onto the back of its unsuspecting prey. While the wolverine is not prone to overeating, it is willing to attack and eat just about anything, including carrion. When hunting, it subsists mainly on small game, such as rabbits or squirrels, but, when desperate, the wolverine will prey on sheep, deer, and even bears and reindeer. Its appetite for reindeer has caused the Sami, who herd reindeer and share the wolverine's habitat, to dislike and even hunt the animal, despite its possible extinction.

In recent years, Swedes have made great efforts to protect the dwindling wolverine population. The species has been protected since 1969, and, now that humans can no longer legally hunt them, wolverines are in danger from no other predator. Despite these conservation measures, the wolverine's tendency to prefer carrion to live prey has made repopulation difficult. In addition, farmers still kill wolverines that stray onto their land.

Above: **The wolverine has a glossy, brown pelt that is highly prized by fur trappers. The pelt is extremely durable and can last through many years of hard winters. The animal also has glands that secrete a strong, musky odor. This odor is used to identify the wolverine to other wolverines, mark its territory, and ward off humans whose food supplies it wants to raid.**

RELATIONS WITH NORTH AMERICA

Relations between Sweden and North America developed in the seventeenth century, when Swedish emigrants traveled to North America in search of a better life. Since then, over one million Swedes have moved to North America. Not only has their labor helped build the United States and Canada into the countries they are today, but iron imported from Sweden was used to build many North American cities and railroads.

Today, North America has hundreds of Swedish organizations dedicated to preserving and promoting Swedish

Opposite: **Founded in 1929 by Swan J. Tumblad, the American Swedish Institute in Minneapolis is a museum and cultural center dedicated to interpreting and celebrating Swedish-American culture.**

culture. These organizations also encourage positive interaction between the nations. Companies that have their foundations in both North America and Sweden flourish, while political relations are positive, with mutual goodwill prevalent between leaders and in trade.

The steady exchange of thoughts, ideals, talent, resources, and products between Sweden and North America, combined with a common heritage of independence and liberty, guarantees that the mutual feelings of goodwill and friendship will continue for many years to come.

Above: **Swedish prime minister Göran Persson (*back row, far left*), Canadian prime minister Jean Chretien (*back row, fourth from left*), and U.S. president Bill Clinton (*back row, third from right*) were among the world leaders who attended a conference on the global economy in Berlin in June 2000.**

Historical Ties between Sweden and North America

Relations between Sweden and North America developed in the seventeenth century, when the Swedish crown became anxious to establish trading links with the New World. As a result, the New Sweden Company was founded in 1637 to trade for furs and tobacco in North America, as well as to set up a colony along the banks of the Delaware River. Swedish trade and the colony lasted only seventeen years before Sweden turned its focus on expanding its territories in Europe.

Sweden turned its attention back to North America toward the end of the 1700s, as the United States struggled for independence from Britain. To pave the way for commerce with the United States, the Swedish king Gustav III sent soldiers to

JOHN MORTON

John Morton's ancestors were among the first Swedish immigrants to settle on the banks of the Delaware River. Morton played a key role in securing the independence of the United States. He became a justice of the peace in about 1764 and was a delegate to the First Continental Congress in Philadelphia in 1774.

Left: This illustration is an artist's impression of Swedish traders negotiating with Native Americans in the early 1640s.

Opposite: In July 1960, Swedish U.N. soldiers were part of an international force that went to Léopoldville (now Kinshasa), the capital of the then Republic of the Congo. The troops were part of a United Nations Security Council resolution that authorized military assistance to the government of the Republic of the Congo. Here, the soldiers are waiting to board a U.S. Air Force aircraft en route to the Congo.

STRAINED TIES OVER VIETNAM

Sweden was strongly opposed to the Vietnam War, and criticism of the U.S. war policy in Vietnam by Swedish prime minister Olof Palme strained U.S-Swedish diplomatic relations until 1974. Ties were further damaged as many U.S. opponents to the war and U.S. army deserters received political asylum in Sweden.

help those fighting for independence. When Britain lost the war in 1783, Sweden was quick to recognize U.S. independence, thus opening the way for trading links between the two countries. The export of Swedish iron soon became the main factor in the two countries' cultural and diplomatic relations.

Since 1814, Sweden has maintained a policy of neutrality, thus eliminating any possible military links with North America. Nevertheless, since 1945, Sweden and North America have shared the common goal of maintaining international peace and security. As the World War II postwar period progressed, relations between Sweden and North America continued to be friendly.

Political relations between Sweden and the United States, however, soured in the late 1960s and early 1970s due to Sweden's opposition to the Vietnam War. This situation, however, had improved markedly by the late 1980s.

Regardless of continued policy differences between Sweden and the United States on some political issues, such as the use of nuclear weapons, Sweden and North America continue to enjoy a strong political and trade relationship.

INTERNATIONAL ORGANIZATIONS

Sweden joined the U.N. in 1946. The United States and Canada had been members since 1945. Sweden, however, opted for neutrality during the Cold War and did not join NATO, which was formed as a military counterweight to the Soviet military presence in Europe. The United States was originally critical of Sweden's neutrality policies but gradually accepted them.

Immigration

Anxious to extend its influence in the New World, Sweden set up its first U.S. colony, known as New Sweden, along the Delaware River in 1638. Established by the New Sweden Company, the settlement stretched along both banks of the river. The Swedish colony, however, was short-lived; it was captured by the Dutch in 1655.

While Swedes continued to settle in New Jersey, Delaware, and Pennsylvania, they did not begin to arrive in North America in large numbers until the nineteenth century. For the Swedes, emigration to North America was an alluring alternative to the harsh life they faced in their homeland. By the mid-nineteenth century, a drastic increase in the Swedish population had brought about difficult working and living conditions. Furthermore, the country was still largely an agricultural society in 1900, with four out of five Swedes living in rural areas.

During the era of mass Swedish emigration between 1867 and 1914, over one million Swedes emigrated to North America, mostly to the United States. Emigration resumed after World

Above: **By the 1940s, many second- and third-generation Swedish immigrants in North America were growing up in their new homeland.**

Opposite: **Saint Lucia's Day is celebrated in Swedish communities throughout the United States and Canada.**

War I, but on a more modest scale, and stopped completely during the world economic depression at the end of the 1920s.

Although the original Swedish settlement in the United States was in Delaware, the Swedes did not confine themselves to the east coast. Following the Homestead Act of 1862, many Swedes began to settle in the west in the so-called Homestead Triangle, especially in Minnesota, which became known as the Swedish State of America. By 1910, more than half of Swedish immigrants had settled in expanding U.S. cities, such as Chicago and Minneapolis, as they strove to move away from farming.

Immigration to Canada first began in the early 1870s, as part of a mass migration to North America. In the hope of acquiring larger farmlands, thousands of Swedish immigrant farmers who had initially settled in the United States moved with other Swedish immigrants to Winnipeg and then fanned out across the Canadian prairies. The period between the two World Wars marked the shift from rural to urban living, as Swedish laborers, along with engineers and businessmen, moved to Canada's major cities. Today, Swedish communities can be found in British Columbia, Ontario, and Alberta and in cities such as Vancouver, Montréal, and Toronto.

LITTLE SWEDEN

Today, the U.S. city of Lindstrom, Minnesota, is known as Little Sweden. The Swedish author Vilhelm Moberg (1898–1973) traveled here to do research for a trilogy dealing with conditions at the time of the first major wave of Swedish emigration to North America in 1850.

THE HOMESTEADERS

Many Swedes were attracted to the United States by the Homestead Act of 1862. This act enabled settlers to obtain the title to 160 acres (65 hectares) of public land if they lived and farmed on the land for five years. Settlers also could buy the land if they lived on it for at least six months and made improvements on it. By 1920, the area of Swedish-owned farmland in the United States corresponded to two-thirds of all arable land in Sweden.

Current Relations

Political and economic relations between Sweden and North America are excellent. Sweden, Canada, and the United States work closely together in many areas, such as the environment, human rights and security, democratic development, and conflict prevention.

The three countries are great supporters of global free trade, and they enjoy profitable trading with each other and other countries. Swedish income from exports totaled U.S. $85.7 billion in 1999, with the United States accounting for 9 percent. Imports to Sweden reached U.S. $67.9 billion in 1999, with the United States accounting for 6 percent. The volume of trade between Canada and Sweden has increased in recent years, and, in 1999, Sweden was the seventh-largest European investor in Canada and the tenth-largest investor worldwide in Canada.

Regardless of political affiliations, Sweden and North America have an active exchange of official visitors and regular high-level government meetings. Most recently, in June 2000, Canadian Industry Minister John Manley and Finance Deputy Minister Kevin Lynch visited Sweden to promote increased business relations through the Canadian Swedish Business Association (CSBA).

Above: In November 2000, Swedish king Carl XVI Gustaf (*center*) was presented with the Lucia Trade Award by the Swedish-American Chamber of Commerce. The award marked the king's continued efforts to support investment, trade, and other economic relations between Sweden and the United States. King Carl XVI Gustaf also works to promote Swedish-Canadian relations. In September 1999, he visited Canada as patron of the Swedish Academy of Science and Engineering (IVA) to study Canadian technology industries, as well as research and educational institutes.

Humanitarian Ties

Sweden, Canada, and the United States are members of various global organizations, such as the U.N., the United Nations Educational, Scientific, and Cultural Organization (UNESCO), and the World Health Organization (WHO), that strive to improve the lives of people around the world.

North American and Swedish troops have worked together on numerous peacekeeping missions in troubled regions of the world. Canadian and Swedish troops were recently assigned to be among U.N. peacekeeping troops who will go to the Horn of Africa to monitor the cease-fire signed on December 12, 2000, by the warring countries of Ethiopia and Eritrea. They will ensure that the area is safe for displaced peoples to return to their homes.

Sweden, Canada, and the United States also play active roles in improving health, health care, and living conditions in developing countries and countries affected by war. At present, all three countries are involved in medical programs to eliminate major diseases, such as river blindness and poliomyelitis, that are widespread on the African continent.

Left: **A Swedish U.N. soldier meets with a Bosnian woman in the streets of Vares in central Bosnia and Herzegovina. Swedish, Canadian, and U.S. troops were part of the U.N. Protection Force (UNPROFOR) that went to Bosnia and Herzegovina, as well as four other republics of the former Yugoslavia, between 1992 and 1995 to monitor the restoration of peace and authority in the war-torn area.**

North Americans in Sweden

North Americans living in Sweden make up a very small percentage of the Swedish population. Most North Americans who go to Sweden, however, are there on vacation, for business purposes, or to study.

The vast majority of North American visitors are of Swedish origin, and they often return to their native homeland to visit family and friends. In addition to family connections, tourism is another major reason for North Americans to travel and stay in Sweden. Stockholm, world-famous ski resorts, and the island of Gotland are just a few of the destinations that attract North American tourists.

Canada and the United States both have embassies in Stockholm. Furthermore, both a Swedish-Canadian and a Swedish-American Chamber of Commerce operate in Sweden. These chambers bring together companies and individuals that are interested in advancing business relationships and trade between North America and Sweden.

Most of Sweden's universities have active student exchange programs that receive North American students. Participating universities include those at Göteborg, Stockholm, and Uppsala.

MINNESOTA DAY

Every year, about ten thousand Americans visit the town of Växjö in southern Sweden; it was from this area that their Swedish ancestors set sail in the nineteenth century. On the second Sunday in August, both Swedes and Swedish-Americans meet in Växjö to celebrate Minnesota Day.

Below: **The Swedish boat** *Talja* **(left) was brought over to North American shores in July 2000 to commemorate the voyage of the Norse Leif Eriksson — probably the first European to reach North America one thousand years ago.**

Swedes in North America

North America's Swedish population plays an active role in promoting and nurturing its heritage through numerous organizations and committees. Some organizations, such as the Vasa Order of America, were established during the mass migration to North American in the late-nineteenth century and helped Swedish immigrants adjust to their new way of life. Today, these and other organizations, such as the American Swedish Institute, promote and foster the exchange of culture between the Swedish and North American communities, as well as celebrate the rich Swedish heritage.

Several Swedish-American newspapers exist in the United States, including *Nordstjernan* in New York and *Vestkust* for Swedish Americans on the West Coast. Swedish restaurants and bakeries are also popular all over North America, as are gift shops offering Swedish crafts, such as glass or textiles.

Recent years have also witnessed a dramatic rise in travel and tourism between Sweden and the United States, mainly due to the Swedish interest in visiting the "new" homeland of their relatives and ancestors.

LUTHERANISM IN NORTH AMERICA

Swedish immigrants played a major role in establishing their religion in North America. The first Swedish Lutheran church was established during the settlement of New Sweden in the seventeenth century. Today, more than 9 million Lutherans live in North America, with the Evangelical Lutheran Church in America having the most members.

SILICON VIKINGS

The Silicon Vikings is a small group of Scandinavians based in Silicon Valley in California. Established in 1997, this group provides a network for people with a strong interest in Swedish technology, business, and finance.

Swedish Screen Legends

Many Swedes have become popular and enduring figures in the world of movies. Born Greta Lovisa Gustafsson in Stockholm in 1905, Greta Garbo was one of Hollywood's favorite leading ladies and later became a legendary recluse. Garbo starred with many of Hollywood's leading male actors, including John Gilbert, in movies such as *Love* (1927) and *Anna Christie* (1930), the movie in which her voice was first heard.

Ingrid Bergman, born in Stockholm ten years after Garbo, was an internationally renowned actress. Bergman starred in many movies and won three Academy Awards for her performances in *Gaslight* (1944), *Anastasia* (1956), and *Murder on the Orient Express* (1974). Her last movie, *Autumn Sonata* (1978), was directed by fellow Swede Ingmar Bergman.

Musical Ties

Dating back to the nineteenth century, Swedish singers have made their name in North America. As early as 1850, Jenny Lind, known as "the Swedish Nightingale," made memorable tours in the United States. Today, Swedish artists continue to contribute to and influence the North American music scene while enjoying widespread success.

THE CIDER HOUSE RULES

Swedish director Lasse Hallström was nominated Best Director for his movie *The Cider House Rules*, starring Sir Michael Caine, at the 2000 Academy Awards ceremony. The movie won two Oscars out of six nominations.

Educational Ties

Sweden and North America have influenced each other in the field of education. Swedish immigrants in the United States founded schools and colleges that emphasize Scandinavian studies and ties with the old country, such as Augustana College in Illinois. Many Canadian colleges, such as York University in Toronto and the University of Ottawa, also offer courses that teach students about their Scandinavian heritage. Several educational foundations, including the American-Scandinavian Foundation and the Sverige-Amerika Stiftelsen, encourage the active exchange of students and teachers among the three countries.

Architecture and Design

As far back as the seventeenth century, Swedish architecture began to form part of the North American landscape with the introduction of a variation of the medieval log cabin by Swedish colonists. Since then, Swedish influence in North America has been primarily in the field of interior design. General Swedish-style decorating is considered sparse but classic and is a style that appeals to many, even those who have no Swedish ancestry.

Below: Swedish king Carl XVI Gustaf (*far left*), Queen Silvia (*second from left*), Crown Princess Victoria (*third from left*), Richard Holbrooke, the U.S. ambassador to the U.N., (*far right*), and others attend the official opening of Scandinavia House in New York on October 17, 2000.

SWEDEN

- A
- B
- C

1

2

3

4

5

NORWEGIAN

SEA

Arctic Circle

L A P L A N D

Muonio

Kiruna ● ● Jukkasjärvi

▲ Mount Kebnekaise
(6,926 ft / 2,111 m)

Torne

▲ Mount Sarektjåkka
(6,854 ft / 2,089 m)

**NORR-
BOTTEN**

N

**VÄSTER-
BOTTEN**

Kjølen Mountains

N O R R L A N D

Åre ●

**VÄSTER-
NORR-
LAND**

JÄMTLAND

Gulf of Bothnia

FINLAND

**GÄVLE-
BORG**

NORWAY

Sälen ● ● Mora

DALARNA

● Sundborn

*Åland
Islands*

S V E A L A N D

UPPSALA

● Uppsala

BERGSLAGEN

VÄSTMANLAND

VÄRMLAND

ÖREBRO

*Lake
Mälaren*

STOCKHOLM

■ STOCKHOLM

Eskiltuna ●

ESTONIA

*Lake
Vänern*

SÖDERMANLAND

Tanum ●

**VÄSTRA
GÖTALAND**

*Lake
Vättern*

ÖSTER-

● Norrköping

● Linköping

*VÄSTER-
GÖTLAND*

GÖTLAND

Gotland

Göteborg ●

JÖNKÖPING

G Ö T A L A N D

GOTLAND

HALLAND

SMÅLAND HIGHLANDS

Växjö ●

KALMAR

LATVIA

**KRONO-
BERG**

Öland

SKÅNE

BLEKINGE

*B A L T I C
S E A*

DENMARK

COPENHAGEN ■ ● Malmö

LITHUANIA

—— County Boundary

■ Capital

● City

⌇ River

POLAND

Above: This fisherman is repairing his boat outside his home in the coastal region of western Sweden.

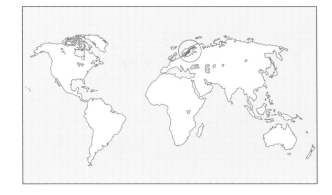

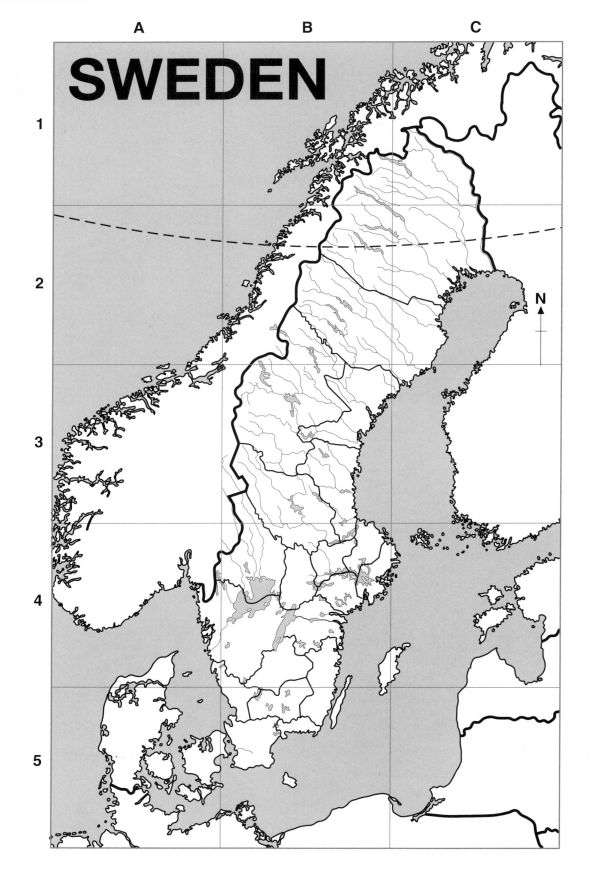

SWEDEN

A   B   C

1

2

3

4

5

N

How Is Your Geography?

Learning to identify the main geographical areas and points of a country can be challenging. Although it may seem difficult at first to memorize the locations and spellings of major cities or the names of mountain ranges, rivers, deserts, lakes, and other prominent physical features, the end result of this effort can be very rewarding. Places you previously did not know existed will suddenly come to life when referred to in world news, whether in newspapers, television reports, or other books and reference sources. This knowledge will make you feel a bit closer to the rest of the world, with its fascinating variety of cultures and physical geography.

Used in a classroom setting, the instructor can make duplicates of this map using a copy machine. (PLEASE DO NOT WRITE IN THIS BOOK!) Students can then fill in any requested information on their individual map copies. Used one-on-one, the student can also make copies of the map on a copy machine and use them as a study tool. The student can practice identifying place names and geographical features on his or her own.

Above: These Swedish girls celebrate Easter by dressing up as witches.

Sweden at a Glance

Official Name Kingdom of Sweden

Capital Stockholm

Official Language Swedish

Population 8,873,052 (2000 estimate)

Land Area 173,686 square miles (449,964 square km)

Counties Blekinge, Dalarna, Gävleborg, Gotland, Halland, Jämtland, Jönköping, Kalmar, Kronoberg, Norrbotten, Örebro, Östergötland, Skåne, Södermanland, Stockholm, Uppsala, Värmland, Västerbotten, Västernorrland, Västmanland, Västra Götaland

Highest Point Mount Kebnekaise 6,926 feet (2,111 meters)

Major Rivers Muonio, Torne

Major Lakes Lake Mälaren, Lake Vänern, Lake Vättern

Major Cities Göteborg, Malmö, Norrköping, Stockholm, Uppsala

Main Religion Lutheranism

Exports Chemicals, iron and steel, machinery, motor vehicles, paper products, pulp and wood

Imports Chemicals, clothing, engineering products, foodstuffs, machinery, motor vehicles, petroleum and petroleum products

Major Festivals Walpurgis Night (April 30)

Easter (March/April)

Midsummer's Eve (June)

Saint Lucia's Day (December 13)

Christmas Day (December 25)

Currency Krona (SEK 9.70 = U.S. $1 in 2001)

Opposite: **Street musicians fill Stockholm's Gamla Stan, or Old Town, with music.**

Glossary

Swedish Vocabulary

Allemansrätten (AH-leh-manz-reh-ten): a Swedish law granting the right of public access.

Dalahäst (DAH-lah-hest): Dala horses; brightly painted wooden horses made in the county of Dalarna.

grundskola (GRUND-school-ah): compulsory elementary school.

gymnasieskola (jim-NAH-zee-eh-school-ah): high school.

högsta domstolen (hohg-stah DOOM-stoo-len): the Swedish Supreme Court.

hovrätter (HOVE-reh-ter): intermediate courts of appeal.

Janssons frestelse (YAHN-sons FRES-tel-seh): "Jansson's temptation;" a layered potato dish with anchovies, onions, and cream.

julottan (YULE-ooh-tan): a special church service held on Christmas Day.

kafferep (CAF-ah-rep): coffee parties.

kommuner (koh-MOON-er): municipalities.

köttbullar (shot-BULL-ar): meatballs.

län (lehn): counties.

Lussekatter (LOOSE-cah-ter): "Lucia's cats;" buns made by mixing bread dough with saffron.

lutfisk (LOOT-fisk): cod soaked in lye.

nämndemän (NEM-deh-men): appointed assistants who take part in Sweden's district court hearings.

ostkaka (oost-KAK-ah): cheesecake made from fresh milk curdled with rennet and topped with fresh fruits or jam.

Riksdag (RICKS-dahg): the Swedish parliament.

Sametinget (SAH-may-ting-it): the Sami parliament in Sweden.

smörgåsbord (smore-gose-BORD): "bread and butter table;" a buffet of Swedish specialties.

surströmming (SOOR-strom-ing): fermented Baltic herring.

tingsrätter (TINGS-reh-ter): district courts.

Västgötalagan (vest-yoo-TAH-lah-gen): Law of West Gotland, a legal code written in 1220.

vik (vyke): bay.

English Vocabulary

abdicated: renounced or gave up a throne, office, or power.

accolades: awards; tributes.

animistic: describing the belief that every part of nature has a spirit or soul.

appropriation: the act of taking possession of, often without permission.

ballast: a heavy material used to control draft and stability on a vessel.

baroque: a seventeenth-century style of architecture and art, characterized by curves and elaborate decorations.

beach: haul or land onto a beach.

Black Death: an outbreak of bubonic plague that spread over Europe and Asia in the fourteenth century, killing a quarter of the population.

caliber: a degree of competence or quality.

confiscate: seize or take possession of something.

consort: wife or husband, especially of a reigning monarch.

deficit: the amount by which the total money received is less than the total money spent.

deposition: a process in which layers of a substance settle and build up on or in something over a period of time.

diplomacy: the skill of being tactful and handling affairs without offending people.

emancipation: the act of being freed from social, political, or legal restrictions.

embroiled: involved in a conflict.

emulated: imitated in an attempt to equal or surpass.

entrepreneurs: people who organize and manage an enterprise, especially a business, with considerable initiative.

Great Depression: a period of world economic crisis that began with the U.S. Stock Market crash in 1929 and continued throughout most of the 1930s.

heel: to tilt to one side.

hereditary: passed on from parent to child.

heresy: a belief or action that seriously disagrees with the principles of a particular religion.

homogeneous: composed of parts or elements that are similar or the same.

indigenous: originating in or characteristic of a particular region or country.

infringe: trespass upon the property or rights of another.

mayhem: rowdy disorder; random or deliberate violence or damage.

municipalities: cities or towns that usually have their own local government.

pagan: related to a religion that worships more than one god.

paramount: chief in importance or impact.

perished: died.

predator: an animal that preys on and kills another animal, usually for food.

provincial: describing a decorative folk style marked by simplicity.

Reformation: the formation of new Protestant religions throughout Europe during the sixteenth century.

relinquished: renounced or surrendered.

rennet: the lining membrane of the fourth stomach of a calf or of the stomach of certain other young animals.

righted: returned to an upright or proper position.

runic: relating to or describing characters of certain ancient alphabets of Germanic languages from about the third to thirteenth centuries.

secession: the act of withdrawing formally from an alliance, federation, or association.

slalom: a downhill ski race over a winding and zigzag course marked by poles and gates.

stipend: a regular, fixed payment.

stranglehold: any force or influence that restricts free actions or development.

suffrage: the right to vote, especially in a political election.

undesirables: people whom a particular government considers dangerous or a threat to society.

unicameral: consisting of a single chamber or house.

viscosity: a semi-liquid quality of thickness.

weather: to disintegrate or change color or shape due to wind, sun, rain, or frost.

More Books to Read

Raoul Wallenberg: The Man Who Stopped Death. Sharon Linnea
   (Jewish Publication Society)

Sweden. Cultures of the World series. Delice Gan (Benchmark Books)

Sweden. Enchantment of the World series. Sylvia McNair (Children's Press)

Sweden. Festivals of the World series. Monica Rabe (Gareth Stevens)

Sweden. Major World Nations series. Ralph Zickgraf (Chelsea House)

Sweden. Modern Industrial World series. Bo Kage Carlsson (Thomson Learning)

Sweden. Nations of the World series. Robbie Butler (Raintree/Steck-Vaughn)

Sweden in Pictures. Visual Geography series. Jo McDonald (Lerner)

Viking Life. Early Civilizations series. J. A. Guy (Barrons Juveniles)

The Viking News. History News series. Rachel Wright (Gareth Stevens)

Videos

Christmas in Sweden. (Spoken Arts)

Royal Families of the World: Great Britain, Sweden, Netherlands, Belgium.
   (Goldhil Home Media)

Travel the World: Scandinavia — Denmark, Sweden, and Norway. (Questar)

Video Visits — Sweden — Nordic Treasures. (IVN Entertainment)

Web Sites

www.gosweden.org

www.nobel.se/nobel/alfred-nobel/index.html

www.sametinget.se/english/index.html

www.utb.boras.se/uk/se/projekt/history/ns4menu.htm

Due to the dynamic nature of the Internet, some web sites stay current longer than others. To find additional web sites, use a reliable search engine with one or more of the following keywords to help you locate information about Sweden. Keywords: *Ingmar Bergman, glassmaking, Gustav I Vasa, Ice Hotel, Alfred Nobel, smörgåsbord, Stockholm, Vikings.*

Index